de book of Mary

BOOKS BY PAMELA MORDECAI

Poetry
*Journey Poem*
*de man: a performance poem*
*Certifiable*
*The True Blue of Islands*
*Subversive Sonnets*

Fiction
*Pink Icing: stories*
*Red Jacket: a novel*

For Children
*Storypoems: A First Collection*
*Don't Ever Wake a Snake*
*Ezra's Goldfish and Other Storypoems*
*Rohan Goes to Big School*
*The Costume Party*

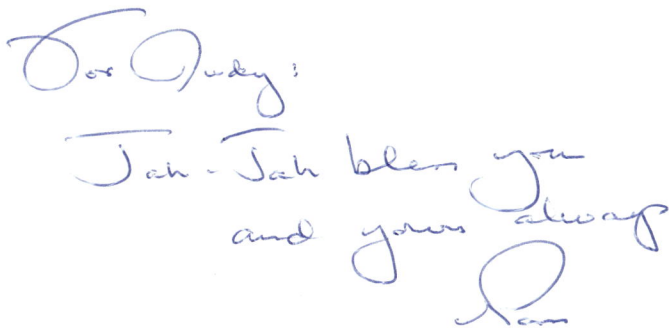

## *de* book *of* Mary

A PERFORMANCE POEM

Pamela Mordecai

MAWENZI HOUSE

©2015 Pamela Mordecai

Except for purposes of review, no part of this book may be reproduced in any form without prior permission of the publisher.

We acknowledge the support of the Canada Council for the Arts for our publishing program. We also acknowledge support from the Government of Ontario through the Ontario Arts Council.

Cover design by Angel Guerra

Cover image: *Maria Full of Grace, 24 x 20*, acrylic on canvas, 2007, by Patricia Brintle.

Reproduced by permission of Patricia Brintle.

Library and Archives Canada Cataloguing in Publication

Mordecai, Pamela, author
    De book of Mary / Pamela Mordecai.

ISBN 978-1-927494-68-4 (paperback)

    1. Mary, Blessed Virgin, Saint–Poetry. I. Title.

PS8576.O6287D42 2015    C811'.54    C2015-905135-5

Printed and bound in Canada by Coach House Printing

Mawenzi House Publishers Ltd.
39 Woburn Avenue (B)
Toronto, Ontario M5M 1K5
Canada
www.mawenzihouse.com

*For Kamau Brathwaite*

*Contents*

*Opening chorus of male and female voices 1*

Miss Ann, Mary's mother, at home 5
Mary, thinking on things, remembers her friend Esther 6
Mary, at home, thinking further on things 8
Archangel Gabriel speaks to Mary 10
Mary, confused 12
Archangel explains 14
Mary, still confused 15
Mary gives Archangel her reply 17
Miss Ann, concerned about Mary 19
Mary tells her story and Elizabeth's news 20
Miss Ann blames Esther 21
Mary takes up for Esther 22
Miss Ann grudgingly agrees with Mary 23
Mary insists she hasn't done anything bad 24
Miss Ann, cross 25
Mary says the baby is specially made 26
Miss Ann gets vexed 27
Mary says that's just how it did go 28
Miss Ann says not to swear 29
A petulant response from Mary 30
Miss Ann, beside herself 31
Mary pleads with Jah-Jah for guidance 32
Miss Beth and her su-su 33
Mary complains 34
Mary tells Joseph she is pregnant 35

*Second chorus of male and female voices 36*

Advised by an Angel, Joseph takes Mary as his wife 40
Cousin Elizabeth greets Mary 43
Magnificat 44
Mary has a baby boy 45
Shepherds flock round the manger 46

Jesus's circumcision  48
Simeon's canticle  49
Anna's prophecy  51
Three kings  52
Mary and Joseph take Jesus and flee to Egypt  54
Jesus grows up  56
Jesus stays back in the temple  59
Mary, as she waits for Joseph to be buried  62
Mary convinces Jesus to perform the miracle at Cana  64
Jesus takes leave of Mary and goes into the desert  67
Jesus disses his family  69
Mary hears about Jesus's ride into Jerusalem  71
Mary watches Jesus condemned to die  74
Jesus is scourged and crowned with thorns  77
Mary and some women of Jerusalem stay with Jesus  79
Jesus gives John to Mary for a son  82
Mary Magdalene addresses Mary's friend, Mariam  83
Mary witnesses Jesus's death  85
Mariam to Mary, as Mary holds Jesus's body  87

*Third chorus of male and female voices  89*

Mary Magdalene brings news that Jesus has come back  94
Mary sees Jesus in the upper room  97
Mary and Leah go with John to Ephesus  99
Mary finds refuge in the hills  103
Mary builds her house on the hill  105
Leah's wedding to Samuel  108
Mary Magdalene visits Mary  110
Mary remembering  113

*Closing chorus of male and female voices  116*

Notes  122
Acknowledgements  124

*Opening chorus of male and female voices*

(*Men in their 40s and 50s, wearing robes reminiscent of priestly garb. Women of varying ages in ordinary clothes. The narration occurs about 48 CE, 18 years after Jesus died somewhere between 30 and 33 CE, and 12 – 14 years after the death of Christianity's first martyr, Stephen, between 34 and 36 CE).*

*Female voices*

(*Addressing the audience.*) Listen, crowd-o-people! Tune in
to dis heartbreak story! Walk a short way
wid dis sistren. Help her bear her load!

*Male voices*

A mythic tale, you hear,
not a thing but make-up
herstory.

*Female voices*

Not a thing but de fact
dat you all ignorant.
Not a thing but dat none

of you lot never carry a child.
*You* all pump us up
so casually

and den for
nine long month
*we* must haul de belly!

*Male voices*

But what dat have to do
wid de matter at hand?
You hail up dese folks,

say you telling story,
den you curse we and talk
about breeding pikni?

*Female voices*

(*Perversely off the subject.*) From de day him born into a stinking stable,
her pikni lay him head like shahaph,
de cuckoo, in a next creature nest.

*Male voices*

Seem like we might as well
go wid your argument
never mind all-o-you

not sticking to de plan *you* propose!
Shahaph de cuckoo, yes!
Him and him barefoot crew was a true loony lot.

Mad master. Crack pupils.
Jesus & Company was a great comedy!
A bona fide paranoid posse.

*Female voices*

Paranoid how? Don't joke! Pharisee,
Sadducee, every power-dat-be
was out to fix de man—

not to mention de humble few
dat ups and follow him
from him preaching begin!

Imagine! Some fellows dat catch fish!
You all not going deny Roman officialdom
downpressing poor colonized Jewry?

*Male voices*

So is politics now? What a way
you jump round like a flea colony
dat have St Vitus dance!

*Female voices*

If de priestman dem never did bribe dat Judas,
no way Pilate send Jesus to be lynch on no cross!
If dem never cook up nuff false witness and lie

through dem teeth, dat injustice would not
come to pass. Is your lot did do it.
Him blood is on your head.

*Male voices*

On who head? After we wasn't dere.
We never response! Is him always mingle
wid trash and rabblement. Him should well

know dem don't have no decency!
He come from David tribe, come from good
family. He should keep wid his class.

*Female voices*

De difference wid Rabboni is *him*
have respect. No mind if is woman, pikni,
outcast wid leprosy, rich or poor,

crazy wid a legion of demon—
him could never care less.
Him bless up everybody same way.

*Male voices*

Old people observe dat if puss
and dog mix, is only to share flea
and spread tick. Plus is nuff

heavy matters we have to look bout.
Best you all choose who tale you telling,
for we don't have all day. So is she? Or is him?

*Female voices*

See? What we did just say?
De lot of you don't have no respect.
Is who you calling *she*?

De puss ma?
Is somebody and *she*
have a name!

*Male voices*

What a yowling inside
a yabba! Fine. She do have a name.
Dem call her Mary.

*(To audience.)* Well, bredren and sistren, Seem is de
bogus virgin we studying . . . Seen?
*(To the women.)* So make we move de story along.

When de tale nearly done
time enough to lament
de birth in de lowly stable, drag out

de tragic crucifixion swan song.
All who fool-fool will stay;
all who have sense will leave.

*Female voices*

And all who want to pitch pikni out
wid bathwater is totally free
to go dem tough head way!

*(Lights down on men and women glaring at one another.)*

*Miss Ann, Mary's mother, at home*

Mary Child, it don't make no point rush
into things without you consider.
No point turning spinner if you can't

twist a spindle, nor seamstress if thread
and needle and finger can't agree.
Better stick to squeeze dough

and make bread! Not dat any girl child
around here have much choosing to choose.
Get betrothed. Set up house. Make baby.

Best enjoy likl freedom while you still free!
Now and den of a morning take ten
minutes and consider. Daydream.

Hear de sigh of your breath. Hear de beat
of your heart. Find a second for non-
sense, for pure foolishness!

Find a next one to laugh, for a smile
is de joy of de world and de joy
of de Lord repeating in your heart!

Not a ting wrong wid dat,
for de prophet himself
Nehemiah instruct: "To be glad

in de Lord is your strength."
Take a pause, a timeout
in de fret of de day.

Look around. Study big
and small things. Read de world.
Figure out de gospel it teaching.

*Mary, thinking on things, remembers her friend Esther*

Dat girl Es, she don't make
not one sound. She don't falter nor flinch
at de sight of a village of ravaging dogs

wid de lust for fresh blood like a fire
up dem tail. Never drop till rockstone
clap her head, topple her to her knees,

shub her flat pon her face. Esther girl,
look de number of time me warn you—
keep away from dat chap!

True is him scrape you up
de day you trip, tumble down,
bruck your nose and mash up

your top lip, almost dig out your eye.
True is him did run quick from centurion post,
snap your snout back in place

wid a smart soldier hand—
dem can doctor real good, people have
it to say, apply ointment, poultice, tourniquet,

guide a babe on him way to de world
safe as any old crone. And is true
him did bring you back home

wrap up in best linen, anointed
and bandaged wid de East finest weave
proper as any high Roman dame!

Make no difference, Es! Time and again
me did caution and caution. You and me
know de same ones coming

wid rockstone so heavy dem well able to knock
out a camel full grown from nuff cubits away,
when de camp fires die down,

don't is dem trading goods,
doing money exchange, parading
dem offspring for de Romans

to long out dem tongue, panting lust
like a pack of bulldog in heat?
Trust Jah! Him will smite dem.

Him don't like hypocrite. But Esther,
you always was somebody couldn't hear!
You always was one set to do other-than-wise.

And me look on you now wid de crust of dried blood
on your limbs like a crackling, a glaze.
And me mourn you, my Es! Feel my arms

in de hug dat dem longing to give your dead flesh.
Feel my breath on your brow. Esther girl,
why you were so determined to go?

*Mary, at home, thinking further on things*

So me taking some ease, like Ma Ann advise,
and me studying a gecko as him climb up de wall.
Is a miracle how de fat creature don't tumble down *plaps*

to him death. And me wondering why
de ancient Rule Book of Leviticus maintain
dat anaqah de reptile is a thing unclean

since him creep on de ground. I don't see
how is fair, since anaqah never
make himself, neither choose how him move,

neither where! Dis one shimmy up
to de roof like him plan to launch off!
Crazy creature! Bird fly and bat fly

and bee fly, and according to Es,
de centurion Marcus Lucullus declare
dat one time in a far foreign land,

him see squirrel fly. But me never hear tell
of anaqah wid wings. Still dem say in dis life
dere's a first for all things.

And dis morning for blue and for light
and for clear is a first time for true.
Me looking from here and de wash

of de waves in de Galilee Sea
as dem rush to de shore,
as dem break, scrub de sand,

hush-hush like de sound
of de boy dem reciting Shema
in de pikni schoolroom next door,

as dem shush, whisper, hiss,
kiss de floor of de sea,
as dem glisten and shine,

is like me and de water is right
side by side in de courtyard just dere,
in de sun of de light, in de white

of de stone warming under my sandal,
gleam of shadow—Oh! Jah! Was just gleam!
Now is gloom! Lord, it compass de room!

A huge hovering thing, fearsome creature, alit
on de air, a shade brilliant, dark glow,
wings spread out, far, far out, everywhere . . .

*Archangel Gabriel speaks to Mary*

"Howdy do, holy one!" A voice sound
all around like it come from deep down
in de womb, in de tomb of a drum.

Cold sweat wash my whole body, same time
big fraid ketch me. I frighten
and shake, hold my breath as I wait

for de far-up-far-down-all-round
speaker to speak. "Child, you fill up de eye
of de great El Shaddai! Out of all

womankind, de plain good
of you quicken him heart. It look like
you same one is to have a star part

in a mystery play him write a script for.
So him send me across de deep black of sky,
a few billion cubits to ask you to be

so good as to grant him urgent plea.
When him talk him voice beat
like a hummingbird wing!

Jah-Jah know is not any small thing him require of you.
Dat is why I am asking you down
on my knees. He say make

sure to ask so, and ask, 'If you please...'
So sweet lady, speaking for Elohim, Most High,
I fly over to ask dat you make a small fry,

fingerling, a pikni dat will wring
every joy from de earth, every ache
from your heart. Your belly

going swell wid Yeshua, Godsend
of de world. But is your choice to make,
is your amen to say.

I am Archangel asking, no mind
dem insist I am Gabriel announcing. Dese earth
creature too love to take

tings and twist to dem suit!
Am-Who-Am-Over-All, De Great One-
Who-Run-Tings, say is choose

you must choose. But for sure he would glad
if you grant him behest and send
me back home wid a 'Yes'."

*Mary, confused*

Well, wid de fuzz from a new baby chick
or de breath of a pikni soft yawn,
you could shub me down flat!

Me don't eat nothing strange, just bread
Ma Ann bake since today, only drink of de well
we custom to draw water from since me born.

Me look on my two hand, my two foot,
count ten finger, ten toe. Touch my nose
just as sure as a bee find a flower.

So me know neither eye neither ear fooling me.
What me see, me perceive; what me hearing, me hear.
De prophet Isaiah will find no fault wid me.

But me still never know what to think, what to do.
Run for Ma Ann? Take refuge in de granary?
Hide my face in de sand like ye'enim?

Manners save me! Me member
a welcome is due to a stranger,
no mind if he come from de stars. So me ask,

"Mr. Archangel, sir, you would like
to sit down? Catch you breath? Have a sip
of water? For it sound like you just

travel here from well far." He say thanks,
he would take a drink, yes. Me go fetch
him a drink. And me scrape up my courage to tell

him de message he bring
is a thing to perplex and confound,
take my head and twist round

for me don't understand
how me going make baby
when me don't know no man.

And me ask how me going to know
wid certainty dat is El Shaddai send him
not no sly Anansi.

*Archangel explains*

Archangel teeth catch sun as he take
a next sip and give out, "Do not fret, holy one,
for de Spirit shall seize you, de power

of De-One-Who-Run-Tings take you in.
Too besides, dem will call de pikni
you going bear 'Son of God'.

El Shaddai going give him David throne.
for David is him forefather long time aback.
And him going reign over de tribe

of Jacob for all ages to come,
and him kingdom going linger
after time been and gone.

Not just dat. Hear dis news!
Your cousin Eliza who bad mind
people take to make sport and call mule

she making baby too—gone six month
already never mind how she wrinkle and grey,
for Jehovah, him do what him please.

As for whether is El Shaddai send
me to you, if you think to yourself,
you will know if is so."

*Mary, still confused*

So me stop and me think but it don't
do no good for me still mix up bad.
When me tell Archangel, him answer

dat is me must make up my own mind.
Him can't get in de way. Me laugh
when me hear dat! "Is true,"

me say. "You can't get in de way.
Angel can't make baby!" And you would
never guess what Archangel reply.

He declare every angel above
in de heavenly host would quick give
dem eye-teeth to bear dis Holy Ghost begot child!

So me forward my next contention
as me make up my face. "Angel don't
have no ma, neither pa to face down!"

Plus me tell him me feel for Joseph, my betrothed,
for him going be well vex. Him say don't
worry bout Joseph, for him love me too bad.

And since Ma Ann and Pa bring me up
to discern and to judge, him suggest
me trust what dem teach me.

"Ma Ann counsel to do what feel right
in my gut. She claim good
sense is dere, alive in my belly."

Archangel, him respond: "Amen! She wise."
So me make bold again to observe Ma Ann don't
have no messenger come down out de sky

wid no burning plea from El Shaddai!
And me further protest she don't have
to worry what bad mind folks going say

as dem watch her belly swelling day after day!
So hear Mr Gabriel: "Wicked folks
bound to find things to chew

dem malicious cud on, gobble spite,
wallow in dem fellow man bad luck,
rejoice when disaster fall on dem!"

Him add, "Is why de baby must come."
Den him raise up him archangel brows and enquire:
"You going make dem decide what you do?"

"No, don't fret bout dat," me assure him.
"But my poor family is God-fearing folks!
Respectability is Bible to dem!"

You think me could persuade Archangel?
"All de more reason you should count
on dem trust! Dem know you from you born!"

So me enquire if him going to stop here long,
seeing as how me should pray about dis, and consult
Pa and Ma and go by de synagogue for de priest advice.

Him announce him must pay
a short visit dis time even though
him enjoy a labrish when him drop in on we.

Den him remind me El Shaddai say,
since is me dat him ask to carry him baby,
me same one must decide.

"Never mind old time ways, never mind
how she young, woman not nobody property.
She free to decide on her own destiny."

*Mary gives Archangel her reply*

Well me more than surprise when me hear
Mr Gabriel say dat. Me regard him and him
look on me as de two of we sit.

Him don't utter one word and me hold
my tongue too. And me pray in my spirit: "Jah-Jah,
show me how me must choose."

And me listen but Jah-Jah not saying nothing.
Verily he leaving de matter up to me.
So me use my good sense and me make a wager.

When few minutes go by, me elect,
wid my courage trembling on my tongue,
to give Archangel my reply:

"Mr Gabriel, sir, seeing as how you explain,
and since I obliging Jah-Jah,
God of Jacob and Isaac and all Israel,

and not doing nothing bad, I can send
my answer. Please tell Him-Who-Run-Tings
I glad him choose me.

And I thank him. And though I well fraid,
I agree. It can be just de way you relate."
And a silence set down as de air

catch a breath and de sun blink
him eye in de bottomless sky.
Archangel, him stoop to de ground

as him say: "Walk good, den, holy one.
And Jah benediction on each breath,
each hour of your days." When him rise,

him make one heap of noise wid him wings
for dem fluffle and sing as him flare
in de air, a black lightning streak,

as him plait de bright rays
of de sun. So me watch him get small
glowing far and more fast

dan de cheetah Lucullus tell Esther one time
him did see on Sind plains. Den de light
of Archangel flash one last flash, disappear.

And like how is Ma Ann me must now tell it to,
me rehearse my reasoning: if I gree and is true,
is not any way wrong it could go in de hands

of El Shaddai himself. If is lie, no harm done.
Never mind what I say, yes or no,
if is nonsense, de whole thing will fade like a dream.

Is a long time did pass before me did learn
Jah-Jah sometimes mean things to go wrong
and some dream can turn into nightmare.

## *Miss Ann, concerned about Mary*

Girl pikni, is where you been hiding?
Me looking and looking
but can't find you no place!

*(She sees Mary.)* Mary child, you looking poorly! Sweat
wash you down! Come rest here
so and tell me what troubling you,

for you look like you see
a army of duppy!
And you walking like you

not so sure on your foot. Best you sit
down before you fall down.
Best you talk. Get it off of your chest,

no mind what de burden.
Don't look so distressed child.
Leastways me can thank Jah

dat is not any crosses like what befall Miss
Rach daughter! Abigail have to hide
way to dickens in Samaria.

You must know how things bad
when de girl have to go and shelter
all dat way, and wid heathen, more so.

But poor thing, she could do no better
for de wretch living in de next yard
advantage de young girl and she making baby!

## *Mary tells her story and Elizabeth's news*

Ma, but why you say dat?
Is like you read my mind!
You going think me crazy but is Jah

truth, I making baby just like she,
so you best conceal me in some far
place like Miss Rach do wid Abby!

Ma, don't look so! Is nothing I plan
and I still don't make out what really
happen in de short time

I spend doing what you instruct.
Is a break I was taking, de same
ease you tell me to take to consider

de world. Dis big angel arrive
and de next ting I know, my whole flesh
is on fire, and my head is a flame

of bright light and my limbs swim and fly,
and I dance wid each creature, laugh, cry,
sing a song wid each leaf,

every tree, every mountain and sea
every small grain of sand. I don't grasp
it, so how I going make

a next somebody know? Me still fraid
till me tremble! See—feel my skin.
It all over in bumps like a just-pluck chicken!

## Miss Ann blames Esther

You? Making a baby? Jah shield me
from de consequence of my gullibility!
Me did feel in my bones dat bad-behaving girl

from next door, dat Esther, was going lead
you astray! Me did check Joachim
and is him persuade me.

Say de pikni never have nobody
at her yard to regard
how she spending her life;

say she was a decent young woman;
attend synagogue, read de Torah
and recite de Shema;

say you would help to settle her down.
But look where trust land me up today!
Me should know better!

Dat damage cannot mend!
Needle can't sew back virgin again—
anyhow dat date pick, it stay pick.

*Mary takes up for Esther*

Ma, how you could talk so?
After Es never lead
me to do nothing bad!

She just hate to stay
inside her yard, just she one,
wid no sis, no bredren,

no mother, neither pa,
not a soul but this one screw face gran
who only can find

fault wid her, never mind
how she struggle to please
de Old Higue. Me know me

shouldn't speak bout a big
woman so, but don't me
must tell Jah truth, Ma Ann?

## Miss Ann grudgingly agrees with Mary

Fine, miss. Have it your way.
Good friend better than shekel,
or so people say.

But my child, don't make joke!
It don't have any way you could get
a baby! You don't leave

out dis house if you don't go wid me—
least not since you betrothed.
Me make sure you stay far

from any man saving for your pa,
and of course your intended, Joseph.
Beg you, Mary, careful, careful what

you saying. People here take dese things
and make life and death rule Jah-Jah self
would not lay down for one living soul!

Give dem a quarter chance
and dem run to establish a next penalty.
Is a barbarous lot dat worship

decree, de vile work of dem wits,
like Israel bow down to de gold calf of Baal
dat dem build wid dem very own hand.

Mary, child, you sure-sure when you talk
dis madness, you certain
you in your right mind?

## *Mary insists she hasn't done anything bad*

Ma Ann, me never do
nothing wrong! Nobody
did force me into any bad act.

No! Please don't tell Pa yet!
You not even going give
me a chance

to report how it all
come about?
Do my endeavour best

to recount
blow by blow,
just de way it did go?

## Miss Ann, cross

What? You think I don't know
how to make a baby?
I was dere to make you,

plus plenty besides you
begin in my belly but never hold on
long enough to reach into dis world.

Your pa did do him share
to increase, multiply and fill up
de earth like Jah-Jah did instruct.

If is you one arrive, is not dat
him or me was confuse bout how man
and woman make pikni!

From Jahweh make de earth
it need two somebody
to make three!

*Mary says the baby is specially made*

Of course me know dat, Ma,
but dis child never make
in de ordinary way people get pikni.

If you give me a chance,
me will try to relate
how de child inside me

come to be in my womb.
But you must promise to
be quiet, Ma, and listen to me.

*Miss Ann gets vexed*

Oh me see! Your pikni
come special delivery!
Must be Jah self come down,

embrace you and proclaim
"Daughter, I, Jehovah,
just give you my baby!"

But me warn you, Mary
dis is not someting you
can play wid. Is your life

in de balance, is your flesh and bone
de hypocrite round here—
dem going only too glad to stone down!

If dem hear dis story
dem going take hold of you
cover you wid a tomb of rockstone!

*Mary says that's just how it did go*

Is just so
it did go,
Ma. Is just

like you say.
only dat
Jah-Jah send

Archangel
Gabriel
to ask me

to say yes
me will make
him baby.

Me say yes,
and is so
it did go,

same as you
just describe.
Believe me,

Ma! In Jah
name, me swear
dat is true!

*Miss Ann says not to swear*

No! You better don't swear!
You well know in dis house
we careful to observe

de commandments of Moses, him law.
So no taking de name
of de Most High in vain.

Mary, you and me know
dat we mostly grow you without licks,
but me telling you now my hand

have a itch just to open out wide,
clap you on your backside
like when you was a likl pikni.

But Daughter, you not no child no more
and a blow on your behind at dis
point in time not going serve no good end—

although Jah-Jah self know
me wish we could get past
your predicament easy as dat.

## A petulant response from Mary

Rabbi say you can swear
in a matter dat shake de earth down
to its root—which mean, I suppose,

not to do it at all for him don't
think a matter like dat will arise.
And it don't just arise in my case,

it stand up, run, lift off, take wing into de sky!
Ma, me can't force you to believe me
but you know me not given to lies.

And if me was going
to dissemble, don't me
would invent a likely story?

You think me would cook up
one outrageous as dis?
Ma, me own-way, but me not crazy.

## Miss Ann, beside herself

Daughter, is one hefty load you lay
top of we. Me here struggling hard
to survive under it

for you know well as me
Deuteronomy state if you making baby
and you don't married yet

for playing de whore inside your
father house, you must stand in de door
of dis dwelling so every last man

in dis town can hurl rock after rock
till you drop down stone dead.
Is three night it take me

to push you from my womb
and me pray to Jah-Jah every hour,
every day, from dat first day to dis,

you would grow up safe
and stay good till you walk
from dis home to your own

married house. And me beg
Jah-Jah send a good spouse
to husband you and all your pikni.

And like spite, as we find
a righteous Israelite, you come wid
dis ridiculous, fool-fool story?

*(A loud rapping from off stage.)*

But is who at de door making up
dat big noise? See here Jah,
we don't need no more crosses today!

*(Miss Ann bustles off.)*

*Mary pleads with Jah-Jah for guidance*

Baby-father, Jah-Jah,
don't abandon me now!
Dis is very rough waters. Steer me

as I go. I have company here
in my womb, no two ways about dat.
As Archangel take off, as him reel

out him wings, my whole body swim in
to de plenty of things, for it hug
up de world, sky and sun,

lake and sea, fish, fowl, sheep,
goat and cow, crawling thing,
bush, flower, tree—

is like all creation living inside of me.
And is not only dat, for it singing a song
and each spurt of my blood

every breath I breathe—
it drumming in time to dat tune.
What growing inside me is not just a baby,

is every last ting! How me going to recount
dat to Ma? Or to Pa? Or Joseph?
Never mind how me try?

How me going to explain dat same time
my body is transported wid joy
it choking wid dread?

## Miss Beth and her su-su

*(Miss Ann reenters.)*

Child, your pa in de yard come to say
a crowd gathering out in de road.
Dat same Beth dat come here

to borrow anyting, from a lamb
to a herd, wheat and oil,
bread and board,

she out dere wid a tale she telling
to all who love su-su. Say she see
a young man jump de wall

to de yard and she hear
you laughing and chatting
up wid him. Say him tall

and handsome. Say she feel
is a real disgrace like how you
are engage to Joseph.

Say is only one thing
she cannot figure out.
Her two eye dem well clear,

yet somehow it appear
de fellow have two something
look like wing sticking out of him back!

*Mary complains*

Baby-father, how you could do we
dis bad ting? We is plain folks, you know.
We don't have no connection wid fat

politician to send to for help,
nor no centurion wid foot soldier
and horse, gladius, javelin

and nuff other weapon
to come take charge of crowd.
And for sure no tribe stay as warlike

as your Israelite dem when dem make
up dem mind for ruction!
But if dem kill me sake of my sin,

is your pikni dem going
to murder before he
have a chance to begin!

*Mary tells Joseph she is pregnant*

Joseph, my betrothed, me don't know
where to start. Me was into de red
of dis egg a long, long time before

me did know de shell mash!
And dere never was egg dat me meet
in my life compare to dis one!

Jah-Jah self know is true!
And is my ma to blame!
No bother look confuse.

It don't mean how it sound.
But is Ma self tell me to make time
to ponder about things.

Is dat me was doing, looking over de plain
listening to de pikni repeating Shema
in de schoolroom next door

when de courtyard fall into
a deep shadow right dere.
I frighten straight away!

And dis angel, big and bright
as de sun ask me if I would bear
a pikni for Jah-Jah.

What I could do? Don't I
must have to say yes?
Don't just stand dere, Joseph,

for you have every right to feel vex
or think me going off my head.
If so, how I could ever blame you?

## Second chorus of male and female voices

(*Lights up. Women are already in their places; the men are shuffling in.*)

Male voices

(*To audience.*) Look like Mary story
turn into a skit, so might as well
play we part, do we likl bit.

Female voices

(*To audience.*) Cho, don't pay dem no mind.
Dem don't have too much sense.
Dem think since dem say so,

de whole Jesus-Jah-son story is
pretense. Dem admit him was here
and him preach and baptize

and de Roman dem crucify him
but dem say de Messiah
and Jah-my-pa part is lies.

Male voices

So how far we did reach in dis tall tale again?
Ah yes! Push come to shub! Mary just
tell Joseph she making a baby. (*They laugh loudly.*)

Better Joseph than any of we!
You would think a man quick
wid him carpentry hand

would have intelligence in him head!
One thing all-o-we done decide:
no way we would married to any woman

wid a next man pikni big
in her belly. Nobody want no
jacket in dem family!

*Female voices*

How you know is jacket? Is one of you grandpa
put de child in her womb? For how else
you could know is not Joseph pikni?

*Male voices*

But don't every soul dere in dat Nazareth town
know de girl come to him wid her belly weigh down?
Dat she breed wid another man seed?

*Female voices*

(*The women laugh raucously.*) Well we must beg pardon for dis
    big buss-out laugh
for de lot of you say is woman love talk,
and is *we* put we nose into people affairs.

So it well amuse all-o-we gossiping hags
dat de su-su bout Mary did spread like disease
from one bad-mouth-man to a next.

*Male voices*

You can go right ahead and confuse reasoning
wid su-su if you choose. From long time we response
for good morals just like we response for good sense.

What a thing when any young woman can excuse
fornication and adultery wid de news
is Jah-Jah offspring dem carrying!

Is we have to save you from gullibility,
faith in nothing more than a pikni poppyshow.
Same thing now, just as two generation ago.

*Female voices*

Good morals and good sense? You must be
making fun. You best remember who
all-o-you talking to.

Nobody here forget Nazareth history.
Nobody here forget who twist
which one story.

Nobody here forget is de high
and mighty who choose how things go.
"Same thing now, just as two generation ago."

*Male Voices*

All-o-you making joke! It could never be we
dat you calling mighty? You all look carefully?
You see anybody look like Roman to you?

*Female Voices*

You name man. Dat is all and dat is everyting.
You is judge and jury. You could stone
any one of we till we dead anytime.

Take dat child, Esther—my gran say
she spend all day everyday
in Miss Ann yard playing wid Mary

and a next girl from on de same road.
De elders in de town did stone
de young girl down like a harlot.

You lot not no better. You all love violence.
Dem cut your navel string
on disruption and war.

*Male voices*

(*Interrupting the women.*) Best you clamp your lip shut for
    enough is enough.
If you keep talking so, you will find dat many
a woman lose dem head to dem tongue.

*Female Voices*

(*Women turn away, kissing their teeth.*) How you all come so
    smart? You proving
what we say! Make we open we mouth likl way
and you gallop to chop off we head!

Come let we go long, yah!
Leave dese sages to see which of us
dem going charge wid what breach of which decree.

Jesus long come and gone. Him did bring
a New Law. It say de likes of you
do not own none of we.

(*Women flounce off.*)

## *Advised by an Angel, Joseph takes Mary as his wife*

Don't a grey head somebody like me,
my helpmate long gone, four pikni,
two son big and married wid dem own family

and two likl girl, should know better?
Tell me why me did think to married
a next time would easy fix my difficulty?

No! Don't take serious thing and make joke.
A wife in a man bed is Jah-Jah provision,
a dream and a blessing,

but two girl pikni wid no supervision
running wild like mad puss
is a father nightmare.

Me did pray, Jah-Jah know, never sleep
plenty night, begging for direction.
When Miss Ann pass my house

wid Mary, me notice how she grow,
turn a miss, not a youngster no more
but a woman graceful as a high

leaping fish in de Galilee Sea.
Same time me sense Jah-Jah
answer to my prayer.

Likl more me and Maas Joachim
agree a bride price. Mary accept me
as husband and put on de veil of a betrothed.

Me smiling content every morning
until yesterday Mary come wid a story
don't make one stick of sense.

Say she pregnant but not wid no earthly baby.
First me think she was sporting wid me
but me sight her mother countenance

and me know is not no fun. When Mary say Jah
send a angel to ask her to make him baby,
my two nose hole flare, my two lip shub out,

and me think to myself, *She take me
for a fool.* Likl most me say so
but me member a rule my old father teach.

"Never speak in anger nor act when
your head hot. Hurry slow to conclusion,
no matter what." So I hold my peace,

listen close, say I must consider
de best course. When me reach home
me put Sarah and Judith to bed.

Me hungry but me too vex to eat
so me walk to de well, draw water,
drink a long cool jug.

Den I pray on my knee. "Jah-Jah, how
you could do me bad so? I love Mary plenty.
If she making a next man baby,

I going spare her de shame. I going send
her far and make up a story about where
she gone off to and what take her away."

After dat my mind give me some ease
so me lay down and sleep.
And a angel appear, clear as day,

bright like sun, and he call me by name.
"Joseph, son of David," he say, "you don't have
to frighten to take Mary, sworn, as your wife;

41

for is de Holy Spirit give her de pikni."
Just as well me was on my back or me would must
fall down! And he tell me exactly

what Mary did say. "She going bear
a boy child; you must call him Yeshua,
for him going save Israel from dem sins."

What to do? Sleepy so, me member
my Mary and me feel it for her . . .
Don't me have to agree to what de angel say?

*Cousin Elizabeth greets Mary*

But is who dis I see coming
cross my doorway? I greet you
likl cuz, full of favour, mercy,

de great kindness of Jah!
My Lord dwells in your sinews; your flesh
is him home. Blessed are you of all

womankind, and holy is de babe
you carry in your womb.
Dat pikni is de fate of de world.

You know how me know so? As me catch
sight of you walking up to de house,
de baby in my womb jump up,

spin around and kick out him two foot!
You will think me crazy but me sure
me hear my pikni laugh!

*Magnificat*

Cousin Liz, see me here
bigging up Jah-Jah. Everyting
in my soul in rapture to know him,

El Shaddai, who rescue me and don't
forget me, no mind me is only
a maid servant to him.

And watch dis! From dis day going on
from one age to de next, every new
set of people will say Jahweh bless me

specially for De-One-Wid-de-Power,
him do great things for me
and him name is holy.

And him kindness is from
every generation to de next
and de next, all as hearken to him.

For him hand well strong and him don't fraid
to make all-o-we know. All who think
in dem heart, dem so high and mighty,

him throw every which way. Him tumble
all who strong from out of dem high seat
and him raise up de poor and de low.

Him provide hungry belly wid bickle so sweet
it make you lick your lip, and him dismiss
rich people—don't give dem a ting!

Him help all Israelite what serve him
faithfully, for him do not forget
to forgive, just like him did promise

to we fathers, Abraham and all him
children going on, till de whole
creation come to finish and done.

*Mary has a baby boy*

Well next thing you know,
de Roman emperor name Caesar
Augustus send out a instruction

dem must count all-o-we!
Dat time in Syria, one man name
Quirinius was governor.

Dem send orders dat every man jack
must find himself back to de town
where him born to write him name

down into a book. So Joseph
set off from Nazareth town where him live
in Galilee country and go to de city of David

what dem call Bethlehem, for is where
him family come from. Him take me
wid him, no mind me big wid baby,

for him say is him response for de two of we.
We leave Judith and Sarah
wid my ma and pa.

At de self same time when we reach
to Bethlehem, dis baby
decide him coming too.

Joseph ask for a room at de inn
but de place pack up right to de brim,
not one likl corner nor crack leave over.

Me sorry for Joseph! Him look high,
him look low till him find a stable and is dere
me born Jesus, wrap him in warm clothes,

give him a first taste of my breast,
and like how we never have no crib, settle him
in de dumb animal feeding box.

*Shepherds flock round the manger*

Den some shepherd, seven or eight of dem,
come round, say dem was in de field
wid dem flock and dem get a big fright

when a angel appear out of a great light
so bright likl most it blind dem.
And because dem did know

is Jah-Jah miracle, dem frighten for so!
But angel smile and say dem mustn't fraid
for de good news him bring

going make people on earth
jump for joy. So of course,
everybody well eager to hear.

Angel say a baby just now born
into David city is Saviour,
Emmanuel, de Anointed One.

And him give dem a sign. Him say dem
going find de baby wrap up tight
in warm clothes lying down in a animal trough.

And same time a big crowd of angel
join up wid de first one. Dem all
praising God and singing,

"Glory to Jah up high in de heavens!
Peace to all down here pon de earth
dat please him!" Talk about a story!

Dem say soon as de angel dem gone
dem set out to look for de baby.
So me show dem my likl boy child,

him face smiling wid sense.
No pikni me know have two eye open so
studying de world right as him born!

All dis while me did glean wid my nose
de liklest shepherd was frighten so bad
him pee up himself. When dem reach,

him did come to de front to look on
de baby, den him hide at de back,
for him shame. So me call him, "Eli!"

(How me know de boy name, Jah to tell!)
"Come, Eli. You want hold de baby?"
When me hand him de child,

him look down on Jesus and him face
catch a fire like somebody strike it
wid a flint. And same time

sweet algum fill de air
all around and boy and baby flare
in a bright candle glow.

*Jesus's circumcision*

When eight day pass and gone
Joseph and me take de baby up
to de synagogue for de mohel

to cut off him foreskin.
According to de Law,
dem have to do dat

to all Israelite man-pikni.
Same time de priest give
him a name. We call him

Yeshua for it mean saviour.
Is de name Archangel
did say we was to give

de baby. Him did tell
me before Jah Spirit
did put de pikni into my womb.

Never come in my mind
to do anyting but
what him say

for, Jah know,
de things
him did promise,

dem wasn't no lie,
nor no dream.
Dem did all come to pass.

*Simeon's canticle*

When time come to cleanse me
just like Moses decree, we carry
we baby up to Jerusalem

to present in de temple for de Law
stipulate, "Every man child who first
open him mother womb, de people

shall take as holy unto de Lord."
Folks like we count every shekel. We
can't squeeze de dunny for a lamb,

so we offer fowl kind to Jah-Jah.
We can just see we way to buy
two turtledove or a pair of pigeon.

Joseph go buy de bird and while me
and de child waiting patient inside,
just de two of we, a nice old man

wid a glow like a haze round him face
come and take de baby out my hand,
hold him close, raise him voice

and praise Jah. "Nuff respect, El Shaddai!
As of now, your servant can go him
way in peace, same just like you did say, for today

me put my two eye on de saving you set up
for every living soul to look on, a light
to show you to all de Gentile dem,

and to big up your special chosen,
Israel." Dis time Joseph come back
wid de two bird him find.

When de old man done talk
my husband look on me and me look
back on him, for we two wondering

about what de old man have to say.
"I name Simeon," him tell us.
"De Spirit of de Lord promise me

I would see de Messiah before
I take leave of dis earth.
And dis pikni I holding is him."

Den him bless us and after dat him
whisper to me, "You see dis pikni here?
Is him same one Jehovah elect

for de fall and de rise of plenty
in Israel, and also for a sign
dem is going to condemn,

so de thoughts in de mind of plenty
people will be wide open to view."
As him look in my eye,

a great sorrow shadow him
countenance. "And a sword
going slice through your very soul too.

Mother of Yeshua,
Simeon heart bleed for you."
And eye-water run down over him

two old cheek and catch up
in him beard, as him take time
and pass my baby back to me.

*Anna's prophecy*

A woman prophet dem call Anna,
a somebody well old, from de tribe
of Asher, arrive at de moment

me take Jesus back from
Simeon. She take one
look on him, lift her hand in de air,

start give thanks to Jahweh
and tell everybody about Yeshua,
meaning all Jah-Jah pikni waiting

for de salvation of Jerusalem. Eye-water
drizzle down from her chin
to de ground in a soft waterfall.

"Mother," she tell me, "look good dis day
on your child, him eye bright, him skin soft.
Put your nose in him clothes.

Smell him clean. And remember him so
on de day him fall down
in de dirt to lift up Israel."

*Three kings*

One day three strange man come to we house
riding on three camel in a trim caravan.
Dem look important and dem dress

like dem rich. Joseph whisper
him sure is three king but me never agree.
Dem more look like priestman to me.

But dat don't signify. Dem recount
a story more strange dan
de shepherd dem did tell about de angel!

Dem reveal dat from far, far away
in foreign, from long time dem was
watching, waiting, searching for a sign.

Den one night dem discover dis big,
bright-bright star and same time
dem give thanks, for dem glad like pikni,

seeing as dem decide is de portent
dem seeking for so long. So dem set
out to follow anywhere it lead.

Dem trail it cross river, down valley,
up mountain, cross plain, for dem know
anytime dem arrive underneath where it shine,

dem going find de newborn baby King
of de Jews. When dem reach
and see me and Jesus, dem kneel

and give thanks to see him. Dem open
dem baggage and take out silver, gold,
frankincense and myrrh, and give Jesus.

Joseph offer dem water to drink. As dem sip,
dem tell him dem did stop by Herod
on de way to enquire if him know

where to find de baby. Herod say
him don't know but if dem find de child,
must come back and report.

Joseph frighten. Him know say Herod
wicked bad. From de three king dem leave,
him face knot up wid dread.

## Mary and Joseph take Jesus and flee to Egypt

When Joseph wake dis morning, him deep
in distress. "How your face come so long
down, husband?" me ask him.

And me laugh and tease him, "Must be a
next visitor come from El Shaddai!"
Him smile soulful, but him don't reply.

"We is helpmate, you know,"
me say as me hug him. "Come tell me
what downpressing you so."

Him kiss teeth. "Wife, you right, as per usual.
Since de three king dem gone yesterday,
angel visit again in a dream, say, 'Get up!

Quick! Take de child and him mother
and make haste to Egypt. Don't leave dere
till I say, for dat evil Herod

looking for de pikni to kill him.'
But beloved, me can't tarry to
give account of de toss and de turn

dat wring sweat from my body all night,
for we have to pack up and move off
just as soon as me feed dis jackass.

Before day dawn, me wake up and hasten
up de hill to ask your ma and pa
to come mind de two girls while we gone.

People fraid out-a-street for dem have it to say
Herod soldier looking for all boy pikni from
two year old to just born.

He give orders to kill dem, every last one!
Is a long journey we have to make to Egypt.
You and me and Jesus cannot spare no time.

We must sneak out quick-quick
just like any tief puss, else dem going
kill Jesus, dead as any dead dog."

So me gather de things Jesus need
and some food and blanket and me climb
top of de donkey wid my pikni.

We walk when is night and sleep when
sun come, like patoo. Was a long
way like Joseph did say but we keep on

till we reach Egyptland. Joseph quick
find employment. Me sew and me bake
and mind people pikni to make life

as we wait on Jah-Jah. And see here!
Is not long before a next angel come
to Joseph in a dream, like last time

wid orders. "Get up, take de pikni
and him ma, go back to Israel
for all dem as was out for murder

dead and gone." Joseph do like Jah say
and we three go back. But like crosses,
was at de same time Herod son

Archelaus take charge, like how him
father dead, and is him ruling in Judea.
Sake of dat, Joseph was well fraid to take me and Jesus dere.

Jah-Jah warn Joseph one more time
in a dream, so we leave and go back
down to Nazareth town

to Judith and Sarah. Joseph fix up we house,
find him hammer and saw,
and we tackle we life one more time.

*Jesus grows up*

Not to say my heart never hurt every day,
but dat boy give me plenty joke too,
sometime make me laugh

till my side nearly buss!
Him did have one black puss.
Where Jesus find dat meagre boy cat,

heaven know! And him tief!
What a animal tief!
Dat puss follow him whiskers to people kitchen,

put him mouth in dem food.
If him hear any sound,
him grab bread, fish, fowl tight

in him teeth, execute a outlaw getaway,
settle down right here next to de porch
den eat till him stomach so full,

it drag down on de ground.
Course it never take long before folks
figure out dat is Jesus puss

taking dem things.
Miss Ruth over next door, is she first
complain to Joseph, say de boy cat

hijacking her lunch. Joseph say
if is true, him very sorry
but him ask if she quite certain.

"But of course," she answer. And she point
to de pile of fish bone on de ground
right beside where de cat sleeping,

belly full of content in de sun.
"Dem fish dere is what me did intend
to eat for my dinner." Hear Jesus pipe up:

"Miss Ruth, why you don't go back inside
make sure your fish missing for true?"
She look on my pikni, kiss her teeth,

huff and puff, but she turn and go back
in her yard. Jesus walk back of her,
take up station just inside her gate.

Likl more, we hear her give out:
"But me don't understand!
When me leave to come over your house,

de fish what me cook and put down
in dis plate, gone way, done disappear.
Now me see dem back here.

Is a very peculiar thing. Very strange!"
And she come back outside and admit
her eye dem did fool her.

When she gone, Jesus bend over, laugh
and laugh and couldn't stop. "Jesus," me ask him.
"Pikni, who give you joke to sweet you all dat much?"

Dis time him and de puss running round
in de yard chasing de ball of string.
Him answer. "Mums, me can't tell you dat,"

and him buss some more laugh.
But from long time me know how dat fish story go.
Him was doing dem tricks from de start!

Not a doubt dat de puss did tief
Miss Ruth food but me sure
when Jesus kotch up at her gate,

him just clap him hand and put de fish
back on her plate. Come evening, she tired
to talk bout how her dinner tasty!

Joseph say we should stop
Jesus from playing dem tricks
but me don't have de heart,

for me never forget what de old man Simeon
prophesy de day him give thanks
dat him see Jesus before him die.

*Jesus stays back in the temple*

When Passover come, de whole family go
up to Jerusalem for de seven-day feast.
Always one crowd of people and one set-o-noise

on de journey dat sometimes take we all five day!
Some walk. Some jog on jackass.
Some bring de lamb or goat kid

dem going offer whenever dem reach
de temple. All day long, donkey bray,
goat kid baa, lamb kid baa, chaos reign.

Pikni romp, big and small. Dem fight when
dem ready and dem howl for buss head or buss knee.
Baby bawl when dem tired or hot or hungry.

Is a riotous jaunt, dat Passover journey!
When Jesus turn twelve, him come
wid him Pa and me and we go like we do every year.

After de feast conclude, we journeying home
in a big company. Jesus, him one
stay in Jerusalem and don't tell nobody.

Joseph and me did think him was wid
a cousin or auntie or gran aunt in de big
crowd of family, so we don't worry until

one entire day pass and we don't
put we four eye on him. We start look.
We ask friend and relation, but not a soul know

where him is! When no mind how we hunt,
we don't find dat boy, we turn back
and we walk de whole way and search

as we going along. But no Jesus nowhere!
Jah-Jah know me vex wid him same time
as me mad out my head wid worry.

"Husband," I say, "maybe a caravan steal him,
kidnap him for a slave?" Joseph shake him head, no.
Jah-Jah not going let nobody tief him pikni.

We ask in de lodging where we stay
for de week. We scrape through every street.
Three distressful day pass, den we find him

in de court of de temple, sitting wid
de teachers, into deep reasoning.
He listen as dem talk. Ask question,

answer when all-o-dem question him.
Everybody dat hear him declare
how him wise, for him well understand

what de teacher dem say, and discuss
wid dem like any learned expert.
Joseph laugh when a man tell him dat.

"Expert yes!" Joseph say. "He come from
out of town." All de same, was no joke.
We don't interrupt, but after him finish talk,

we tackle him. Me ask Jesus straight,
"Son, why you treat us so? Pa and me
look all bout, never find you at all!"

Me could see Joseph getting ready
to clap him, when dat pikni give out,
"You was searching for me?

Don't you know one day me
would must have to look after
my Father affairs?" Joseph eye

make four wid Jesus own. Him caution,
"Jesus, is true we minding you sake
of Jah-Jah, but better you don't do

nothing like dis again!" Jesus drop
down him eye but him don't
answer back. Is a long time before

me did grasp what dat whole business mean.
Meantime me carrying all dem things
in a thread bag resting on my heart.

*Mary, as she waits for Joseph to be buried*

Him was plenty year older than me
when we did get married. Him two big son
gone dem way wid dem own family

but him still have two young girl pikni
tumbling round in him house. Sarah, de likl one,
she is seven, and de big one, Judith, she is ten.

Dem did well need minding and is dat
make Joseph consider to married a next time.
All now me cry eye-water telling de story.

We make life together and raise Jesus,
Judith and Sarah for more than half of my
time on earth, thirty-five year.

Before me meet Joseph, me did spend
every day in de temple at Jerusalem,
for is dere Ma and Pa take me when

me was small, and vow me to serve Jah.
Me stay dere till me reach to fourteen.
Den de priest dem decide me must leave

Jah service, and dem tell de high priest,
Zachariah, is time me should go.
No, me say. Me not breaking my vow to Jah-Jah.

Zachariah, him never did know what to do,
so him pray and beg Jahweh to guide him.
Jahweh say call all de widowers dem in de land.

Him do what Jah instruct, plus him tell dem
make sure bring a staff when dem come.
My Joseph, may Jah welcome him to paradise,

him arrive wid de rest. When dem reach,
Zachariah take way all de staff dem and go
in de temple and pray. When him done

him come out and give back everybody dem staff.
What a palampam! Nobody can figure out
what going on. Den just so

a dove fly from out Joseph staff
and sit down on him head—
so dem know him and me

was suppose to married.
Me give thanks dat Joseph live to see
de two girl settle down

with two decent young man and set up
on dem own. Is fifteen granpikni
dat him bless before Jah call him home!

Jesus and me did know Joseph was sick bad,
so me make sure to weave him three shroud,
and Jesus build him coffin timely.

Him cry as him plane cedar plank
and shape dowel pin and glue
de wood box for him Pa.

Jabez dat live next door, me did have
to ask him run go tell Jesus say him pa pass,
for Jesus working in a next yard.

Jesus anoint Joseph, wash him clean, trim him hair,
bind him in de three shroud. While me wait
for de wailing woman dem to come, me think bout

how dat child change my life, turn me into scandal,
baby-mother and wife, exile in a strange land,
wid Simeon knife de whole time digging into my heart.

### *Mary convinces Jesus to perform the miracle at Cana*

"Listen Jesus! De people dem run
out of wine." *What a crosses!*
*me thinking in my mind.*

"Jesus! Son! You hear what me saying?
Dis party just begin
and de people wine done!"

*Me raise my voice loud-loud but Jesus can't hear*
*for him on de far side of dis yard.*
*Me shout louder.*

"Son is me! Over here! Is your Ma!"
*Him still don't hear a word!*
*Make me move likl closer for not even me*

*can hear myself talking in dis noise.*
"Cry excuse! Beg you please
give me pass? Me need to get through

to dat man over yonder, him
wid de beard." *Okay, See me right here*
*side of him. Him must can hear me now!*

"Jesus, me telling you de wine done.
Down to de last dribble. Son, you don't
hear what me saying to you?"

"Woman, dat don't have nothing to do
wid neither you nor me, for my time
don't come yet." *Well dat one*

*surprise me.* "But my son,
how you can take up dat attitude?
Look how much stranger come

wanting dis, begging dat
and you don't turn down one?
Look how much time me watch

you peel clothes off your back,
give to strays on de street,
feed nuff hungry belly?

How come you now decide you
not concern wid dis situation,
'for your time don't come yet'?"

*Him just look on me. Don't say nothing.*
*Him plainly in one of him moods, so*
*me going just do what me have to do.*

"Listen, servers. A word, if you please.
Kindly do as dis rabbi instruct. Never mind
what him say, just follow him orders."

*Sometimes me think my son is crazy.*
*Can't think why him asking dose fellows*
*to fill up de big water jar dem*

*dat wash hand and wash foot.*
*Is not water dat finish, is wine!*
*But see here! Is what dat pikni doing?*

Now him tell de server to draw
from one of de big jug and take to
headwaiter. Headwaiter take time taste,

den him call de bridegroom.
"Master, how you come so contrary?
Everybody me know when dem throw a party

share de best wine out first,
bring de bad when de guest dem so drunk
dem can't tell de difference

but you keep de good wine
for de last." De bridegroom well mix up.
Scratch him head. Can't make no sense of it—

just well glad dem don't have
to feel shame. But Jah-Jah,
is now I realize why my son

never want to make a miracle dat day.
Someting change from dat hour.
Like a weight descend

and seize him down to de bone.
Oh my son! Why your Ma
couldn't leave well enough alone?

*Jesus takes leave of Mary and goes into the desert*

Plenty hard to believe my son turn
thirty dis winter season just gone!
Not dat me never watch

every minute, each day, as him grow.
But is like you see and you don't notice,
and den, all of a sudden dis big

somebody hold your face in him hand
kiss you on you forehead,
say, "Mums, I going now."

Never mind how much time
I protest and ask why him must go
off, him one, to a place wid no water, no food,

not a green thing to lift him spirit . . .
"Mums," him say "why I would
leave dis house, you and Gran, best cook food

in dis town, my sistren and bredren,
and de whole family, plus de woodworking, too,
all I love, if it was up to me?"

I breathe deep, gaze on him
from him head to him toe, one last time.
"See three loaf of new bread I just bake

in dat bag, and a wineskin your gran
send wid Judith daughter dis morning.
She say, send, tell her when you going."

"I going stop by de yard
as I leaving, to tell Gran goodbye.
Big thanks for de eats and de drink,

but you know my food in de wild
going be fasting and prayer, my Mums.
I sure you don't want my papa up so . . ."

and him turn him eye up to de sky,
"to vex wid me right as I start out?"
"Why you can't pray here, son?

I will keep food and drink far from you.
I will honour your fast. Is a thing I do for
Joseph plenty times when him was still wid us."

Him bend down and kiss me,
say, "Mums, dis not de worst.
Me must get ready for some dread tings."

When I go to answer, him put one finger on
my lip. "Hush, Mums," him repeat,
"believe me, if de choosing was mine

I would stay."
And him look round de room,
touch de big water jug, scuff de rug

wid him foot, take him staff
and walk through de door—
never turn him head round to look back.

## *Jesus disses his family*

Jesus was in a house wid a big
crowd-o-people pressing down pon him,
de horde of dem shouting "Hosanna!"

Dat time we know de scribes dem
was out to capture him. Dem figure
to trip him, say him break Moses Law.

Me and him bredren come and we stand
up outside and we send to call him.
No surprise de back row

turn dem ears to fast in what is not
dem affairs. "Listen, Jesus!" dem shout
when dem see us, "You know your mother

and all your bredren waiting outside?"
Well me know whatever
him answer, it going cause ruction,

for every circumstance is a time
for teaching, and him come determine
to mess wid people mind.

"And is who is my ma, or my bredren?" him ask.
As we watch from outside, we see him
stand up, look round de crowd,

left and right, and we hear him declare,
"All of you is my ma, my sistren
and bredren!" Same time a su-suing

travel through de gathering
and me feel every eye swivel round
to measure how my countenance stay.

"Anybody dat do what God say,
dat one is my bredren,
my sistren, and my ma."

And Jesus find my two eye dem
wid him own. Him look straight
in my face, and him wink.

*Mary hears about Jesus's ride into Jerusalem*

Is de tale James did tell when we meet
up wid him. We was waiting wid food
to feed Jesus dat day. When we see

so much folks come wid him to de town,
we frighten. John call him bredren, James, and Andrew.
"Make we look for a place for de Master to eat."

Den John go fetch Jesus for we did think him was
teaching de gathering all dis time.
While we wait, James relate de story.

"When we getting near Jerusalem and we reach
to Bethpage, to de Olive Hill place,
Jesus send two of we wid orders

to go to de town coming up next on de road.
Him say we going find a mother ass tie up
wid a colt. Him instruct we to untie

de two animal, bring dem come
back to him. If anybody fuss,
him say we must tell dem,

'De Lord need de two beast!'
and dem will send dem straight, no delay.
Two of we go and do just as Jesus command.

When we bring back de jenny
and likl donkey, everybody start peel
off dem garments, throw dem over de ass

and de colt so de Master could sit in comfort
as him ride. After dat, de massive
fling dem clothes on de ground

as de Lord riding past. Some chop down
branch from tree, take dem cover de road,
so Jesus could ride over dem,

a green carpet to Jerusalem.
And de crowd up in front
and de people behind shout out, 'Hail

to de son of David! Blessed is
him dat come in de name of Jah-Jah!'
'Praises be to de heavens on high!'

When Jesus reach to where he could see
de city, he stop and regard it
tender like woman gaze on pikni,

and he cover his face, and he weep.
'My city, my city! Make you couldn't hearken
to de gospel of peace?

Now it not dere no more. And de day
not far off when your foe going ring you
round wid war works and dash

you and your pikni down
on de ground. When dem done, not a stone
going to stand on a stone.

All because your neck too stiff to confess is me
who is visiting you.'" As me try
to make sense out of James story,

John come back, but no Jesus wid him.
"Too much folks! Dem all want
to find out who dis Jesus is. De crowd

push and shub, swarming to reach near him.
Dem as know telling all who don't know:
'Is Jesus! A new prophet from Nazareth town

down Galilee way!'" Den John halt,
take him two hand and cover him face.
When we ask what happen, him say:

"De crowd bad, but de real trouble is de Master.
Him in de temple mad as any rabid dog,
throwing out de sellers, roaring dat scripture say,

'And my house is to be a dwelling of prayer
but you take it and change to a haven for tief!'
Jah-Jah know him don't have not a chance

after dis. Is detention, and prison and Jah
know what else, for dem not going make him
get away wid disrupting anyting name trade."

*Mary watches Jesus condemned to die*


It hurt me when me think is just few day pass
since Jesus come to town on de ass
wid de whole Jewry making up noise,

waving palm and shouting to de top
of dem voice, "Hosanna to de Son of David!"
But is so politricks stay, safe today—

tomorrow at de mercy of ungodly men.
Mariam come in distress and find me.
She say in de garden over Gethsemane

him was keeping watch wid him friend dem
when one whole heap of soldier and ragamuffin
grab ahold of him and haul him off.

De hard part is Judas come and kiss him to show
which one dem is to seize. And is him
same one swear dat him love Jesus best!

Me and Mariam check wid de rest of woman
and we make up we mind we staying wid him,
don't care what wickedness dem cook up.

If it come to dat, dem can kill all-o-we too!
And we find we self to de palace of Pilate
to watch Jesus facing de governor.

Pilate ask him, "So you is de king of de Jews?"
"Don't is you same one say so?" Jesus
answer back. Den de chief priest dem come,

and de elders dem come and dem charge
him wid dis and wid dat—all pure lie!
Him don't say not one word.

Pilate ask him, "You don't hear de witness
dem bring against you?" Jesus mouth
still lock tight, so surprise Pilate.

Me frighten for my son like how him
know full well de malice of de priest dem—
Pharisee, Sadducee, de whole bad lot of *see*!

Every Passover time, de governor was use
to let go a prisoner dat de massive choose.
Round dat time dem did have a criminal name

Barabbas lock up into de jail. When de crowd
of dem gather, Pilate put it to dem:
"Tell me which one you rather me to let go:

Barabbas, de murderer, or Jesus
who you call Messiah?" Pilate know
was dem own evil ends dat make dem

carry Jesus to him. (One devil know de wiles
of de tribe!) My heart dive in my belly when me
see de chief priest and de elder dem run

up and down in de crowd, coaxing dem to ask
for Barabbas and make Pilate condemn
my innocent son. When Pilate ask again:

"Well, which one you want me to give you?"
don't de whole of dem scream, "Barabbas"?
"Den is what me must do wid Jesus

who you call Saviour?" When me hear de question,
de sword Simeon warn me about cut right through
my tripe, sharp like a butcher-man blade, for me know

what dem going to demand. Me tremble all de same
as dem shout like a pack of hyena greedy
for a corpse, "Crucify Yeshua. Crucify Yeshua!"

"But what crime him commit?" Pilate now insisting.
(Me don't trust him. Him good to hide tricks
in de skirt of him robe!) Is like Pilate don't talk.

De rabble just baying, "We say crucify him!
Nail up Yeshua de Nazarene!" When Pilate
realize dem not going change dem mind

and dem just getting more and more rabid and wild,
him take water and wash him two hand.
"Hear me now!" him sound like him vex.

"For me want you to know dat is not
*me* response for de blood of dis innocent man!"
Who him think him fooling? All-o-we know if him

want free Jesus him just have to turn up him thumb!
"No Master! Never fret! Is not you, sir! Is we!
Responsibility for de blood of Yeshua is on

all of we! And on we pikni, and dem pikni pikni!"
So Pilate set Barabbas de criminal free,
release him to de heap of howling

mad Jewry, give him soldiers dem
orders to flog my one son,
and to crucify him when dem done.

*Jesus is scourged and crowned with thorns*

Den dem drag Jesus into Pilate
judgment hall and dem gather a legion,
one whole battalion of soldier around him.

Dem strip off him clothes, and wrap him in
a purple cloak like him is a king,
twist together some macca to make

up a crown, jam it down on him skull
so de prickle dem sink in him brain.
When me see it, me likl most lose my temper,

for me quarrel wid Jah-Jah when time me ready.
*Baby-father, tell me why is not dem to dead?*
*Why my blameless pikni?* Me watch dem

shub a staff into Jesus right hand,
and den kneel and make a fool of him.
"Hail, Yeshua! We salute you, King of de Jews!"

De brutes dem spit on him, grab de rod
out him hand and lick him in him forehead—
not one time, again and again like de devil in dem.

When dem done, dem drag off de bleeding
robe, dress him in him clothes and haul him
out on to de Golgotha roadway.

We cry living eye-water, de sistren and me!
We hold on hand to hand, stumble behind Jesus.
When he turn round and see us he say:

"No bother waste eye-water pon me.
Bawl for yourself; bawl for your pikni.
For de time is coming when people going to say,

'Blessed are all who don't have pikni, de womb dem
dat empty, de breast dat no baby ever suck.' At dat time
dem going plead wid de mountains, 'Fall on top of us!'

Dem going beg de hills, 'Cover us, please.'
For if human being behave like dis when tings green,
how dem going carry on when tings dry?"

Me come stand up where he can see me,
and he whisper, "Mums, don't cry.
Is so it have to be. Is why Abba send me."

*Mary and some women of Jerusalem stay with Jesus*

Dem did mangle my son, butcher him back
wid whip. It so bad, when dem done
you don't see skin or flesh, just a bright

red morass dat so meke-meke it paste
de purple cloth on to him. When dem tear
it off and put him clothes on again,

him tunic hide a ripe crimson sea.
Jesus, child! Just as well is Jah-Jah beg me bring
you down here. Dat alone is my sorry excuse!

When dem look on my child after all dat abuse
dem figure is no way him could heave
dat back-bruck gibbet reach top de hill.

Dem lucky. As dem shub Jesus out
on de road dem buck up a fellow from Cyrene
name Simon and dem collar him to help Jesus.

Sun well hot, not a breeze raise a breath—
only creature stirring is de army of fly
escorting my son, flying into him eye,

getting drunk on him blood till dem plap
on de ground like black olive, ripe
full of juice. Is not dem alone drop.

Jesus tumble down too, never mind him have help.
Two, three time him fall down, and for each
time him fall, de soldier dem whip him

like a dumb animal. Is so him and Simon
take de hill, first one step, den a next,
not a shoes twixt him foot and de hell fire stone,

make me wonder who tief him sandal!
Dem travel, and we go long wid dem, till dem reach
a place name Golgotha, "de skull-pan of a head."

And is dere dem hammer him two hand
to de wings of de cross, set one foot
top de next, drive one spike through de two

set of bones, nail him down to de wood
like a warning. Den dem raise de tree,
drop it into de hole, and him groan

as de crash ravage flesh in him hand
and him foot. Dem hang two criminal
side of him, one to left, one to right.

Likl more me hear him telling de
soldier dem, "I-man need some water."
Is bad mind make dem bring vinegar

and give him. Him taste it but him refuse to drink.
Dis time him rib-dem bruck and dem jooking
him chest, every heave dat it heave.

And me scream to Jah-Jah for me vex to de root
of my soul. "Lord, me cannot believe dat is dis
me born your pikni for! El Shaddai,

is how you so cruel to your own?"
When dem satisfy wid how dem plant de cross,
dem stand back and draw straw for him clothes.

Big fight nearly pop, for dat long shirt, it weave
in one piece, have no seam. Me did make it myself.
All dis time dem sit on dem rear end guarding him.

Now, tell me how a body dem maul so, den nail
on a tree could need any watchman?
One take hammer and chisel and a piece

of deal board, like him writing notice.
When him done him climb top a rockstone
dem roll near de cross, nail it up.

It say, "Yeshua, King of de Jews." And like spite
as de massive dem pass, dem insult
my pikni, bawl out "Majesty!

"Don't is you dat did say you was going
mash down de temple, build it back in three day?
Make you can't save yourself? Make you don't

fly come down, if is really Jah-Jah son you be!"
So dem mock him, down to de chief priest and elder.
"Make him save so much people and can't

save himself! If him is really King of Israel,
make him find him way down! Like how him
is God Son, why him Father don't rescue him now?"

*Jesus gives John to Mary for a son*

Don't know why but my spirit don't take
to dat John chap at all. Is true
him one of de lot of disciple

wouldn't leave, stick wid Jesus till now,
stay right down to de last—though talk truth
him don't have too much use

for him don't make no protest,
don't put up no fight. Him just move
when dem shub him to left and to right

while is not a few kick dat de girl
Magdalene land on nuff soldier shin.
One of dem take a spear

and him jook she and me, and she
double her fist, fix him good
wid a thump. Him let out one loud squeal

and Jesus raise him head
and nod when him observe what transpire.
"Dat's my girl!" him breathe out on a sigh

(me barely could hear what him say),
"for I come wid a sword to set man
against man till de lot of you figure tings out."

Is a contrary fellow, Jesus, my pikni
for him well know long time how me feel
about John, but de one him just say

me must take for my son, de person
him appoint to mind me like him Ma?
Don't is him John same one?

## Mary Magdalene addresses Mary's friend, Mariam

Me tell you, Mariam, if you live long enough
you see plenty strange tings! See me stand
up here side of him ma, water jug on my arm,

bag of bread at my side, wineskin sling
round my neck, me de strumpet, me de whore,
me de one dem decide carry clap

from de camp to de whole holy town!
When she see me first time, him and me,
hand in hand, she give me a cut eye

would slice through any crocodile skin.
"Don't mind Mums," him did say. "She looking
out for me. You have to understand.

Me is her so-so son!" When me hear dem arrest
him, me never think twice. Me grab water, grab wine-
skin, grab ointment and bread and me head

out de door. And me know dat no mind
how him mother look at me, me going wid him.
She could like it or not.

And you know, when me bounce into her
in de press, she hold on to my hand like a leech.
"Is you wash him two foot wid eye-water?

Dry dem wid your hair?" Me nod, yes.
"Him say every tear drop help wipe fear
from him heart. De warm wrap of your hair

moor him will like a rope lash a boat
to a post, so it ride out a storm.
Him say when him journey over miles

and him preach, teach and heal,
and dem mock and jeer him for reward,
de oils you bring help ease him sinews

and bones, ease de ache in him soul
and de burn on him skin. And him say
dem sin gainst you plenty more dan you sin."

And I cling on to her and she hang on to me,
and just so, don't is hand holding hand
how de lot of we drag we foot come

up dis hill? You and me and him ma,
Veronica and Ruth, and Elizabeth too,
and Martha, don't is we walk wid him

from dat rodent Judas bring de priest
and de soldier dem come
to de Garden of Gethsemane?

And except for dat John what him love
specially, look and see! Don't is just
pure woman around dis rootless tree?

## Mary witnesses Jesus's death

Den story come to bump.
From middle day, darkness
descend upon de land.

And same time Jesus holler,
"Eli, Eli"—My God, my God—"Why you
leave me here, me one all by myself?"

When some of dem hear,
dem laugh and dem declare,
"Him calling Elijah!"

One go find a old sponge, fill it wid
vinegar dat make out of palm wine,
hoist it up for Jesus to drink.

De rest say, "Now leave him
by himself. Make we see
if Elijah come down to save him."

Likl after de ninth hour pass, Jesus scream
from him bottommost heart,
"It done now!" and him let go him life.

Same time earth start tremble
and de rock dem explode.
De tomb dem in de cemetery

bruck apart. When de centurion
and de rest of soldier
guarding him

feel de earthquake and see
all de dread happenings,
dem so frighten, dem bawl out

"Him was Jah Son for true!
Yeshua was Jah son!"
We woman stay same place,

never leave we station,
Mariam, Mary Magdalene and me,
and de rest of we friend.

And we give thanks to Jah
at long last de wickedness finish
and Jehovah get back him one son.

## Mariam to Mary, as Mary holds Jesus's body

Dat Aramaic him speak was gutter talk,
same like de koine Greek.
Him wield dem two and de Hebrew—

sound clash was always on him tongue.
You disremember how him give you lip
at twelve going on about him pa affairs?

Nice slap in Joseph face! Me guess him
did figure if you drop down dat day
from heart attack when you never find him,

him would just speak three word
and restore two of you to hale and hearty!
Still, Jah know, one son or no one son,

if him forget himself, bring me dat
forwardness, is plenty licks
on him teenage backside!

Proverbs say, "Whoever love him son
does chastise him betimes."
Destined to cause many

to rise and fall in Israel, indeed!
Is all dose things go to him head
make him think him could jump

in Big Man Politics, him and dat
ragtag bunch. Is plenty time dem stop
by my cook fire when gas full up dem belly

and beg me for a lunch! Complain him
send dem out wid nothing but a staff—
not a crumb, no bag, neither money

in dem belt, tell dem, stupid chaps, to
"Trust your fellow Israelite to give you
bed and board." Is crazy dat him was,

or fool-fool? Is de same countryman dem
dat him heal, feed, baptize
and promise living water, plus

a new kingdom dat don't have no end—
don't is dem string him up?
"Give us Barabbas, de murderer!

Crucify Yeshua de Nazarene!"
Respect due, all de same.
Him wasn't one to look askance

and let advantage-takers get away
wid foulness. You know de girl dose
Sad-you-see and Far-I-can't-see hypocrite

was hell bent on stoning? You know is
one of dem misuse her, den run back
and report how she slack?

Me don't know if somebody tell him,
but him one face dem down,
and never break a sweat.

Sorry! Sorry! Mary, my love! I
babbling because like how him lie
down breathless, lifeless into your lap,

no mouth on him no more, no hand to
clap nor spittle to mix up wid mud
to make a miracle, me feel me should

say some small thing to comfort you.
But in de end all me bring is words
me borrow, de last ones

him speak: Tetelestai! Like how
him dead, de work of dat sword of grief
Simeon promise you—don't it done?

*Third chorus of male and female voices*

(*Women are onstage. Men are assembling in their places.*)

*Female voices*

(*To audience.*) But what a brutal, wicked thing!
Imagine! Priest conspiring
to murder?

And a blameless man at dat!
Sacrifice him to keep
dem share of Roman power!

Him mother, poor creature!
She cry out her two eye.
In de end dem run red like her son.

(*To the men.*) And is only a high
holy crew such as you
could set it up so good!

*Male voices*

Like we say already,
none of we was present
at dat luckless event.

*Female voices*

Luckless? Luck never have
no part in dat intrigue!
If ever a murder was plotted

and designed, engineered
wid a scheme of pure evil in mind,
it was butchering Mary one pikni.

*Male voices*

Hold strain, girls.
Take it easy. No point
falling off de deck. If you play

drama queen we not going
get nowhere. Make we keep
things in check!

*Female voices*

(*Interrupting, irate.*) "Girls?" You can't be serious?
De youngest one of us
is mother to seven pikni!

*Male voices*

Man can't make likl joke?
Is so you bruise easy?
Well, all right. We sorry

for we never mean any offence.
We will call you lady—
woman if you prefer!

*Female voices*

Don't bother to come now
wid any "likl joke"!
We look like we laughing?

And it don't matter what
name you choose
to call us,

for all-o-we know
who talking
down to who.

*Male voices*

All right. Have it your way.
De point is, if you study de tale,
if you look at it fair,

you will have to admit Mary son
did pretty much ask dem
for dat crucifixion.

*Female voices*

(*Sarcastic.*) But of course! Is stupid we stupid!
Him did want dem to kill him.
Him was counting on it.

Him was dead set on one
of him twelve apostle sneaking off
to betray him to dem devilish priestman.

Him was glad when dem hatch
a villainous plot to entrap
him wid blasphemy hot on him tongue!

What a comfort to hear
him friend Peter declare
him don't know no Jesus—

never buck him up yet!
What a pleasure to meet
Caiaphas, Ananias, Pilate!

What a treat
to listen to de mob
bawling out for him blood!

And of course,
what a splendid climax
for him mother to watch

wid de rope
of de cross
round him neck!

*Male voices*

Scorn is what people use
when dem know
dem going lose.

*Female voices*

Well, we never set out
to have no argument.
We was hoping you could

in all fairness agree
Jesus never do nothing
to deserve such abuse.

*Male voices*

Tell de truth, dem did deal
him some rough punishment.
But we must consider

circumstances back den,
view de situation
wid de eyes of de time.

*Female voices*

Well de eyes of de time
must be blind to de very last one,
for de man never do nothing bad.

*Male voices*

Just like every monkey
think him offspring pretty, woman view
dem pikni wid a mother soft heart.

*Female voices*

Who you calling monkey?
And you all can go-long wid your
"mother soft heart"!

Dem capture Mary son.
Set up one of him friend
to sell him master out;

send out spy;
spin nuff lie,
use a outside army,

foreign politician,
arrange Jesus death by
Roman dispensation.

Never have de guts to
do dem own
dirty work.

What a vile,
worthless set!
You should shame!

*Male voices*

*We* should shame?
How we name
get call in dis preke?

(*Men throw their hands up, bewildered. Lights down.*)

*Mary Magdalene brings news that Jesus has come back*

Is Mary Magdalene did come wid de story
dat dem lost Jesus! Say him just disappear.
Say she go to de grave, see de stone roll away,

no sign of him body nowhere. So she run
and search for Simon Peter and John.
Two of dem come, go into de grave,

and find de clothes we bury him in.
But when dem never see no trace of de Master,
dem turn and go back to dem yard.

She one stand dere crying and crying,
till someting say to her go back
and take a next look inside de grave.

And, Jah help us, she see two man dress
up in white shining like two angel
sitting on de ground same place where

we did lay Jesus down. One sit at him head top,
de next one at him toe. When dem see
her, dem ask "Woman, why you crying?"

"Dem take way de body of my Lord, Jesus,"
she reply. "And me don't know is where
dem put him." When she turn

back walk out, she catch sight of a man
and him ask her, "Woman, is why you
crying so? You looking for someting?"

She did think dat him was de gardener,
so she answer, "Please sir, if is you
take him way, beg you tell me which place

you put him, make me go fetch him back."
When he smile and say, "Mary!"
same time she know is him. She bawl out,

"Rabboni!" and she run up to him
but he hold up his hand to sign stop.
"You can't touch me, Mary, for me don't

go back up to de Father as yet.
I rather you go to de bredren, tell dem
I say 'I going back to my pa and your pa,

my God and your God.'" Magdalene,
she make haste find de bredren and give
dem de news. She say she sure dem think

she was mad, for her full head of locks
flying out all about, and her foot
dem cover wid de dust, for she don't

stop and wash, just gallop in de house
bawling out at de top of her voice,
"Bredren and sistren! Is me, Mary,

Me just see Rabboni! Him come back
from de dead! Him raise up like him say
and send me to you wid a message

about him Father!" She tell dem what Jesus
say to her. Den of course is a long
questioning, where and when and why-for,

till she get vex, declare she don't care,
dem could believe de message or decide is lie,
make no difference to her.

After dat, she hurry up here, run inside,
shouting out like pikni, "Mary Ma!
Where you be? Where you be?"

When me come from de garden round back
where me grow one, two things,
she drag me in de house and she grab

my two hand and repeat and repeat,
"Him raise up, like him say. Him come back!
Mary Ma! Is Jesus! Him come back!"

And two of we hold hands
as we cry and we laugh, and we laugh
and we cry, and try as we try, we can't stop.

*Mary sees Jesus in the upper room*

If Mary Magdalene never put
her two hand round my waist, hold me up,
me faint *flups* pon de floor.

Is not dat me never believe he would raise
from de dead, for in all of him life, Jesus never tell lie.
And is mostly dat why me did take it as fact

when he say he was going to come back.
Plus of course, how me was to forget
Jairus girl pikni, or Lazarus what he raise?

Furthermore is *Jah-Jah* wish him into my womb.
His hand was in dis right from de start
and he not one to do things half way.

Still when Jesus appear—
*braps* one minute not dere—
*braps* next minute in de midst of we,

my heart fly from my bosom and kotch
in my mouth! And him look so different
when me look on him face and him form.

First thing, him look so clean wid no spot
to remind of de blows and de bruise
and de battering dem deal out to him.

Den him open him hand
and me look in de red of de wound
(not a crust, not a scab, kosher dry)

and recall how him structure did jump
and drag down on de nails
when de cross did drop into de hole!

And me gather de jolt in my body again
for me certain is him choose de cuts
to remain as a sign

of de cost of de cross,
as a love bite bright into him skin.
And me think, *What a business, dis sin!*

True, dat signify, yes, but it was
of de least consequence,
for de rest of him look

same way as de day him did born,
like a light beaming out,
like him body could barely contain

de self of de somebody inside,
like as if already he
was in a next place,

far from here. Me recognize him
as de child of my womb while me don't
comprehend him at all. He smile and

his mouth form de word, "Mums."
Me smile back and open my arms wide
but he shake his head. No.

"Peace, bredren and sistren,"
he say. "Peace unto you." And me feel
de room fill wid de deep of de sky

on de day de archangel did fly
from eternity into my father yard
and put question to me.

*Mary and Leah go with John to Ephesus*

One evening John reach here blowing hard.
"Mary Mother, make haste! Move quick-quick!
De bredren insist we must leave now,

else Roman official and bloodthirsty rabbi
going arrest we, imprison we, stone we to death
like dem murder we bredren, Stephen."

(Stephen dat first follow Jesus
to de grave for speaking God truth
to Sanhedrin. Dem priestman get blind vex,

so dem do what dem know to do best,
pound him bones to powder.)
Me tell John, "You forget today not

de first time me run way."
(Me and him turn good friend
since Jesus gone back up to Jah-Jah.)

"Dis history commence wid a long
banishment to Egypt. Remember?
So things change, so dem stay like before."

So me tell John all right, and as night
finish mop up de sky we set off,
me and Leah, my maid, riding top

two jackass wid de few thing John say
we can bring. John him sporting a staff,
say him going on foot.

And we lock we lip tight.
Not a word as we tip on we toe,
take a step, den a next, den a next . . .

Just as well, for de evening clear as a chime.
Not a fly stir de air. We can hear
every sound, soldier drowsy around

dem campfire drunk as rat-bat
on moonshine, talking slack, telling who
dem subject to what wicked misuse.

Me just whisper soft-soft de Shema
me learn from de boy school next door
when me was a young girl.

"Hear O Israel! De Lord our God, Him is one."
And just like de first when Jesus,
Joseph and me run away to Egypt,

we walk while is night and we rest
in de day. And dat John!
Take him nose smell a cave

in a hill or quarry like him is any dog.
When sun ready to rise and get rid
of de dark and we stop,

him tilt him beard up, lift him two
hand shade over him eye, move him head,
side to side, sniff and sniff.

Den him point and him say, "Mary Ma,
make we search over so,"
and we find a hideout without fail.

We feed de two donkey and de three
of we catch likl sleep. After four
whole night pass, and three day,

me ask John one morning where we going,
for till now him don't say. "Is a long
way, Mother, over dry and wet too.

But for now we pasting we eye
on dis road de Roman dem build.
We going follow it from a ways off

till we reach to de sea." "And which part
dat is going to be, John?" "Caesarea," him reply.
"It will take two more day, maybe three.

As soon as we arrive, we will seek
for a boat to take we de rest of de journey."
Well, me don't like dat part but me never tell John.

Me and water don't gree. Me don't like
travel sea, not even to sail in de small canoe Peter
and him bredren use on Galilee Sea.

Jah bless us for we find a small group
of Jesus believers when we reach
Caesarea, just five, but dem give

we de best bed and bickle and travel advice.
One Aaron, a fisherman remind me of Pete,
say him son, Jonah, have a vessel

go and come from here up de coast to Antioch.
Him say in dat city dem have plenty big ship
dat sail far, to Perga, Miletus,

even to Ephesus, for is dere John declare
him taking we. "Far and safe, Ma!
We fleeing from Jerusalem!"

So we sail wid Jonah up to Antioch and
him find we three place on a barque
ploughing waters to Ephesus.

Lucky thing Jonah make we practise how to sway
and to swing while we still on firm ground
so it never so bad when we rock on de waves.

Not to say three of we never lose we breakfast!
Me joke bout it wid Jesus, for me
talk wid him in my mind every day,

*My Jesus, is not just one way sufferation
come upon human flesh!*
And me turn up my belly again.

Was a long, long time until we gain
Ephesus and find de home church dere.
De bredren and sistren take we in

but we never stay long, for John say
best we hide up de hill.
"Too much talk in a town.

Better keep we head low.
Roost wid fowl dat know best
to mind dem own nest."

## Mary finds refuge in the hills

So one morning early we set off
for de hills wid a young man, Samuel,
who come from up dose parts.

Was no easy climb wid de sun
sizzling but a stream soothe de land
every turn of de road and de earth

bear fruit like a good wife, for we see
olive grove, maize and millet and peas,
pear orchard, and some citrus tree too.

Now and den de wet ground and green grass
call out to we foot, "Take a rest!"
When de sun nearly capture de top

of de sky, a girl child, maybe six,
gallop down a steep track bawling out,
"Samuel, Samuel!" She run direct to him.

Samuel scoop her up, spin her round,
kiss her one, two, three time,
set her down on de ground

wid a grin sliding into a laugh.
"Is Rachel dis, my sis. So she small,
so she bellow like any bull cow! Likl girl,

why you always make so much noise?"
She grab on to him, turn her head
back to where she run from, and we see

a tallawa man, slim woman, and about
five pikni clambering up de slope in a line,
waving like is old friend dem greeting.

So we spend time wid Samuel and him family,
help dem plant, tend garden, mind goat,
sheep and cow, and look after pikni.

John, him don't tarry long for him have
to return to Ephesus to build up de church
and to water de faith in Jesus

but him promise to visit, hope to come back soon.
And we laugh and assure him, like how de place strange,
and de hillside well steep, we don't have nowhere going!

*Mary builds her house on the hill*

When it get wet and cold and we mostly inside,
dat time we know is plenty of we! Samuel
and him ma, him father, three sister,

three bredren, him grandma, plus Leah,
also me, and a dog and two cat
and a bird always sing in a cage.

So when next John come visit, me tell
him we best try locate quarters
to suit Leah and me.

John agree so we start to look round
wid de help of Samuel family. We ask in
de district, we walk and we look.

One day we was searching,
cloud cover de sky thick and dark,
frowning like dem so vex

any minute dem going spit, when me hear
a bird call and turn round to de sound.
Truth to tell, as me eye sight de flat

on de hill, me did know is dere
me will spend my last days.
All de same, me just stop

on de track and stand back,
take my time gaze on it and listen
for de voice of my son in my heart.

*Go on, Mums. Take it slow and walk up.*
*It not hard to reach dere never mind*
*de path looking so steep.*

*And it have a stout stream flowing through,
faithful as de new day for it run and don't stop.
Plus a quarry not far, so stonemason can dig*

*out all de stone him need.
He too sweet, my Jesus!
So you set, my Mummy!*

Me laugh as me turn back
and me holler to John
"Make we walk go up so!"

Just as Jesus describe, just so it turn out:
easy slope, steady stream, stone quarry,
and it all sitting down in a wrap

of bright green. "Is right here,
John. Right here is de place.
We don't need nothing big—

just a small house of stone
we can dig from de hill over dere.
Me and Leah will help carry dem.

And me know to lay stone.
Joseph never do only carpentry work;
him do masonry too and me watch

as him teaching Jesus and me learn!"
"Seems you have it all figure out, Ma!"
John smiling, "but we must find out who

own de spot you want to build house on."
Turn out dat was de simplest part.
Seem de village did set aside land

for widow and cripple and orphan,
one piece here, a next piece over dere.
Me tell dem like how Leah don't know

neither pa, neither ma, for dem dead
from she small, and like how Joseph pass
from before Jesus did turn twenty,

it look like two of we qualify!
Plus me promise if anybody in dese parts
turn cripple, whether can't walk or talk,

lose dem hand or dem foot or even lose dem mind,
dem can come share we space and
whatever we have. So all of we agree.

And give thanks house build fast,
for wet time never turn
good to dry

before Leah and me
pack up pot, pan, and poe
and take up residence.

*Leah's wedding to Samuel*

Did sweet me how Samuel set him heart
on Leah while she and him and me
dragging rock from quarry.

She never dream him have intention!
Since her parents dem dead and she don't
have no kin, when him ready to ask

if she can married him, is me him come to.
Me tell him, by rights, so we give no offence,
him should take him enquiry to John.

And what John could do but say yes?
And so we arrange for de ceremony
of betrothal in de stone cottage on de hill.

John and me stand up wid Leah when
Samuel show us de solid terms
of de marriage contract.

Him propose de bride price of a ram and a ewe,
never mind John advise him never
have to pay, seeing as her ma and pa long dead.

Den Samuel spill some wine in a cup
and sit frighten waiting for Leah
to drink up, which she take her time do,

wid her eye on de ground and a grin
from one ears to de next. Once him know
she consent, him tell her,

"Me going to my yard to fix a place for you.
Me come back for you when it ready."
Leah smiling so broad she weary her mouth!

According to custom, Leah start wear a veil
everywhere to show she engage to Samuel.
De boy work like a ant for de next

thing we know, him and all him friend dem
walking in a long line on de track
dat wind up to dis house. Of a sudden

dem stop and dem blow de ram horn
to signal dem come to collect her.
Was a wedding send my mind back to Cana.

(Me still pondering if my son life
would go another way if me never beg him
to help out when de wine did run short.)

Come time for bride and groom to retire
to dem honeymoon room, family
and friend sing, play tambourine and dance.

When Samuel friend come out
and announce de bride and de groom is
become one in de flesh,

de whole company start to rejoice all de more,
and de serious eating and drinking begin.
What a fête and commotion and noise,

for dem dance and dem prance
and dem sing till dem hoarse.
Me don't stay till de last all de same.

Me pick my way by a shy moonlight
up de track to de house on de hill
and linger on de porch, for me still

take a pause now and den to consider
de world, never mind one morning
it did set me on such a strange road.

*Mary Magdalene visits Mary*

When last John climb dis hill him announce
Mary Magdalene coming to Ephesus and
she dying to see me and visit my house.

Not a soul in de church
going refuse bread or board
to a stranger much less to a friend of Jesus.

Plus Mary is special to my son.
She stand by him cross down
to de last! Furthermore any sin

dat she sin, she repent it long time.
(Too besides, who is dere without sin,
like Jesus did enquire. When him want

to tease me, him declare as soon as
dose word find dem way out of him mouth,
him remember me, and say a prayer

me wasn't nearby. "Not dat you
would fling stone—right my Mums?"
And he chuckle just like when he small.)

So I fix de room Leah did use and I wait
to see John and Mary Magdalene.
Soon as Mary see me, she leave John

side and run to greet me, and I hug
her tight-tight, and I feel a tear travel my cheek.
Me tell her "Mary love, please don't cry!"

"But I must, Mary Ma," she say,
"for I don't see you since tongues of fire
descend on de bredren and sistren

in Jerusalem." John share bickle wid us
but him leave right after for de night
was moonlight—good to follow de track down de hill.

Next day Mary and me visit Sam and Leah
for she bring some things for dem pikni.
When we walking back up to de likl stone house,

me hear sniffing, turn round, see Mary wipe her eye,
for me walking in front of her, leading de way.
"Mary dear, what troubling you?" me ask her,

and she wave her hand over de hill
"You don't see? It look like Calvary,
like de walk to de Hill of de Skull."

So next day we return down to Samuel house
and we trace Jesus journey up to Golgotha.
We remember de fellow Simon from Cyrene

dat did help Jesus carry de cross.
We recall all de times him did fall
to de ground, how de soldier dem

whip him and drag him back up
and we howl, two of we, like pikni
when we think of de nails and de long

punishment in de sun, how him give John to me,
forgive de criminal hanging on de next tree,
how him bawl out "Abba, how you forsake your son?"

When we reach home we sit and give thanks
for Jesus, and de good news him bring,
and de Calvary cross, and de blood

him bleed for all of we. "You know
Mary Ma, we should mark out de way
Jesus carry him cross on dis hill

to recall de journey." So de rest of her visit,
she and Samuel and me pile up stones
to mark every step Jesus trudge to him death.

Long after Mary Magdalene gone,
de bredren from de Ephesus church still coming
up dis hill to remember Jesus on de way of de cross.

*Mary remembering*

From he stand on his two likl foot dem
and walk, Jesus love a ball. His gran
did use twine and make one

and Jesus and de tief puss gallop
round de yard running after dat ball
de whole livelong day. Jesus do

as we say but him love joke for true.
One day a old rabbi pass by de yard
and see Jesus playing wid some bird

him use mud and construct.
De teacher call out, "Yeshua! Stop!
You toying wid idols and breaking Jahweh law!"

You should see de man mouth
greet him knee when de flock flap dem wing
and fly off! We did have plenty fun,

my Jesus and me, and him papa Joseph.
He grow sturdy and strong and Joseph
learn him good, and he help his father

wid de carpenter work. Never fail
to hearken to whatever we say—
well, most time anyway!

Funny how is de start me want to recall
now me come to de end. Don't protest
John, my son. Make no sense

call a thing by any but it own rightful name
and is not like me fraid to go back to Jah-Jah.
Is my Baby-father after all!

Me can see it so clear! From de day
Angel Gabriel fly down, when de sky
was as clean as de heart

of my bad-lucked cuz, de Baptist, preaching
all-o-we was in need of redemption, so we
should repent, promising somebody was going come

after him, somebody so holy John never
deserve even to bend and unlatch him sandal.
And dat somebody was my pikni, my Jesus.

De old man, Simeon, just as well
him did warn about de misery my baby
was going to set off in my life.

Was a easy mistake to think Jah
would supply a plain way
for me and him pikni to traverse.

Yes, me know. Me not staying one spot.
My mind chasing all bout like Jesus
and de puss running after de ball.

But you know de story I rejoice to recall
is de tale of dat palm-branch Sabbath,
and dat royalty journey to Jerusalem.

Jesus come on de scene
riding on dat jackass like a king
wid him retinue strolling longside.

John is you-self did tell de story—or is James—
when we waiting for Jesus to finish preaching,
and come sit down and eat?

And you go to find Jesus and come back and say
him in de temple raising Cain? Make me go
slow and cast my mind back, for is plenty years pass.

Sky was deep blue dat day, not a blemish of cloud.
Sun hot but a breeze blow and stop, blow and stop.
Put me in mind of how so much people

did say dem love Jesus and den turn against him,
how plenty who cheer him did end up
bawling out, "Crucify de Nazarene!"

Funny how every memory lead to dat cross,
like it was de whole plan, a scheme
Jah-Jah did mean to end bad from de start!

Beg you pass me a cup of water, John my son.
My lip dry till dem crack. Dis fever
like it sucking de last bit of juice from my bones!

Talk de truth, I tired to be sick,
to trouble you and Sarah next door
and Samuel girl children dat fetch things

from market and bring wood for de fire
when time cold. Is whole night you been here?
Why you don't go back down to Samuel?

Get some rest? Me all right by myself
for de next likl while. Me feeling me need
some shut-eye, a nice long dreaming nap,

so don't bother rouse me if me sleeping
when you reach back here. Me will wake
in good time, Jah-Jah time.

*Closing chorus of male and female voices*

*(Men and women in their places as lights go up.)*

*Male voices*

Make we done argument,
end dis disquisition
on a make-up virgin

wid a dubious tale.
We done waste
enough time already.

*Female voices*

Don't know why Mary story annoy
you so much?
Is your conscience, maybe? Is because

you feel shame? But *you* never kill him.
You declare it a likl while back.
None-o-you is to blame.

*Male voices*

Back to Jesus again?
What rot all-o-you brain?
How much time we must say

is de mother story
we recounting today?
Is you all set de course.

*Female voices*

Like we say already
parenting
not someting

you have insight about.
Mary no have no story
wid her pikni leave out.

*Male voices*

If it wasn't for she, true, him would
never born. You know how much discord
and disruption him cause?

How much chaos him one occasion
wid him stupid good news?
A fine king of de Jews—riding one jackass!

Stumbling to dat vulgar display on de cross
at Passover! Bringing we high holy days
and we ancient tradition into disrepute!

*Female voices*

She did take a brave plunge.
Have pikni and him grow,
turn big man, collect up a dozen

ordinary folks and send dem out
on de road wid a message of love
and forgiveness and peace, feed a crowd

here and dere, preach a sermon or two,
do a likl healing, den die on a cross.
Whether rise or don't rise don't put food

in your gut nor roof over your head,
so it hard to know why, after dis
long time pass, you all still in a stew

about what de man say or did do
or not do. And is her story, yes,
but her son is de star.

*Male voices*

Every good Jew man know de Law say
take a eye for a eye and a tooth
for a tooth, fair and square.

Den dis fellow arrive telling folks
if tief take dem tings,
dem must not take revenge,

saying turn de next cheek
when a man take him hand
and box you cross your face!

Plus him run wid low-life
and make a mockery of de faith
of we fathers, dem rule and decree.

*Female voices*

But how dat affect you?
What it can have to do wid de price
of fresh fish in de market today?

*Male voices*

Don't play like you stupid.
Just like *she* proclaim she well glad
to be ma for Jah-Jah one pikni,

same time as she mourning
dat a knife cut-cutting through
her inside, won't stop—

now how dat could make sense?
Same way dis man capsize
de way we been conducting affairs

from we roam wid Moses
through de wild, and him bring
Jahweh Law write on de two tablet.

Nurture your enemy?
Forgive who do you wrong?
Dat can restore Israel?

Make we nation strong?
Who him think him is?
Moses or Elijah?

*Female voices*

Story have it to tell dem same two did appear
on a hill top near here and dem chat wid Jesus.
Him did shine like de sun. So dem say.

Den Jah-Jah voice proclaim, "See my son
who me love! Hear what him telling you!"
Three apostle was dere. So dem say.

*Male voices*

Superstition. Hearsay.
People like make up story, invent
every kind of marvel.

*Female voices*

Have it your way. Okay. But him stick in your craw.
You all choking on him while you hold
on to Torah, and Prophet, and Law.

*Male voices*

If it wasn't for him, woman like all-o-you
would never lose dem pass interfere
in matters beyond what dem pea-brain

can manage. Not a thing but mayhem
and madness ensue when people
do not know dem right place.

Man is man. Man in charge.
So Jehovah ordain.
So de Torah declare.

Your Jesus dead long time.
We run things as of now.
Who have ears better hear.

*Female voices*

What you all going do?
Stone we down wid rockstone?
Crucify we for de whole world

to see? You think people stupid?
Dem will quick figure out dat authority—
meaning you reverend folks—

couldn't manage we poor
likl female posse! De whole town
and country and empire going hear

you can't keep good order
in your yard. *You* going see
how quick *you* lose de work.

*Male voices*

Exactly why dis Yeshua business
must stop. She come wid her one son
miracle baby—for she still a virgin—

wid Jah-Jah as him pa!
Him say him is a king but him have
no riches, no subject, no territory

for him "kingdom is not of dis world . . ."
paradoxically! But den dat
is him trade. Treat your enemy good.

Forgive all who wrong you.
Love your neighbour who turn
out to be every old

sore-foot man, every stink bag-lady.
De man was off him head.
Your Jesus was crazy.

*Female voices*

Old folks say you can lead
jackass go a water
but you cannot oblige

him to drink. At de risk
of imprudence, you lot
and jackass

have a good resemblance.
You think tings
going
roll
back?

*(The women laugh and walk off singing the Jamaican folk song, "Woman a heavy load . . ." Lights fade on the men looking pompous, indignant.)*

# Notes

## Names of God

The names of God as represented in this text are several: Am-Who-Am-Over-All, De-(Great)-One-Who-Run-Tings, De-One-Wid-de-Power, Elohim (God of Gods and the name for God used most often in the Old Testament), El Shaddai (God Almighty, God-Who-Blesses), Jah, Jah-Jah, Jahweh and Jehovah. As a general rule, Jah and Jah-Jah are the names by which ordinary folks refer to God, reserving Elohim, El Shaddai, Jahweh and Jehovah as names used by rabbis, priests, holy persons, prophets, angels and ordinary people who are reporting or imitating the speech of such persons. For example, Archangel Gabriel uses the names El Shaddai and Elohim, and prompted by his example, Mary on occasion uses the name El Shaddai. In addition, Mary once or twice uses the name, Baby-father, to refer to Jah-Jah as progenitor of her child.

## Names of Jesus

Similarly, the name Jesus is used privately, at home, and the name Yeshua, publicly. His family calls Jesus by that name, while the holy man, Simeon calls him Yeshua.

## Location, Culture, History and Bible Story

I have taken liberties with physical space. For example, the Sea of Galilee cannot be seen from Nazareth or nearby Seforis, where it has been suggested Mary might have lived her early life with Ann and Joachim. Land and sea journeys are, however, projected according to maps of the time, and based on actual voyages.

Not a lot is known about many of the simpler aspects of Jewish life in the time of Jesus. Nevertheless, where there is information, I've tried to be fact-faithful, preferring Jewish shekels to Roman denarii, though both might well have been in use, and having both Mary and Leah wear veils once betrothed. In describing the annual journey to Jerusalem for Passover (prescribed in Exodus and Deuteronomy) as being made by Mary, Joseph and their extended families, my assumption is that they were strict observers of this law. By the Second Temple period, the injunction was not stringently applied.

Though there is differing information about the punishment for adultery in Jesus's time, what Miss Ann says to Mary on the matter is by and large consonant with Mosaic Law. I have gone along with the sources maintaining that because Mary was betrothed, her becoming pregnant for someone not her contracted spouse would have been adulterous. The punishment for adultery was that both parties were to be stoned in a public place. It was perhaps an injunction more honoured in the breach than the observance, given the extent of polygamy and the keeping of concubines in the Old Testament. Leviticus, Numbers, Kings and Chronicles appoint stoning as the standard form of judicial execution. "All the people" were expected to participate.

As for the Bible story, where scholarship indicates a difference with tradition, I have mostly ignored the scholarship. Thus, though some scholars suggest Jesus was born in the upper (sleeping) chamber of a home in Bethlehem, I preferred the location of a stable. One example in which the text does respond to scholarship relates to the Christian portrayal of Pilate. I owe JonArno Lawson thanks for pointing out that, though Christians have seen Pilate in a somewhat sympathetic light, history suggests otherwise. According to Josephus, he was ordered back to Rome after the Samaritans reported him to the Legate of Syria for attacking them on Mount Gerizim. There were complaints from the Jews as well. In the first soliloquy in *de Man* (published in 1995 and last book in this trilogy), Naomi, a maid in the retinue of Pilate's wife, has the measure of Pilate, whom she describes as a frog-face having "neither/Character nor courage/Nor the commonsense/Fi do what him wife seh."

*Language*

This book is not written in *very* creole Jamaican Creole (JC). It slides across the JC continuum, being acrolectal or Standard Jamaican English on occasion, but mostly operating at the mesolectal or middle level. Thus, sometimes the subject pronoun *I* is used, and at other times, the JC, *me*; sometimes the subject pronoun *he* is used, and at other times, the JC *him*. It was a source of much distress not to be able to use the JC plural form of you, *oonoo*. I chose not to use it because it would be unfamiliar to non-JC speakers, and increase the challenge of understanding the text. But it was sorely missed.

*Orthography*

I thank Jean D'Costa, Mervyn Morris, Velma Pollard and Olive Senior for advice about how to represent JC without using the Cassidy-Page or any other strict orthography. Bearing in mind non-JC speaking audiences, I have suggested rather than represented the sounds of the language mostly by changing *th* to *d*, where appropriate. *Th* is changed to *t* only in cases where it occurs in particularly flavourful words, such as *tief*, and also *ting(s)* in emphatic contexts. I have also used non-English JC words, such as meke-meke, macca, patoo, preke, tallawa. In one or two cases, where JC words are used, they are explained in the text. Where they are not explained, the context in most cases supplies the meaning. Finally, in the same way that I felt free to use both English and JC pronominal forms, I have used both English and Creole forms of words like about (*bout*), and agree (*gree*).

# Acknowledgements

First, sincere thanks go to the taxpayers of Ontario, who, through the Ontario Arts Council Works in Progress and Writers' Reserve programs supported the writing of this book. I thank my husband, Martin, especially, for being my reader/critic/consultant in a patient and ongoing way. Without him, my writing would be an impossible undertaking. I am grateful to Marlene Bourdon King, George Elliott Clarke, Jean D'Costa, Stan Dragland, Thomas Glave, JonArno Lawson, Rachel Mordecai, Pat Penn Hilden, Timothy Reiss, Barbara Sheppard, Jennifer Walcott, and Betty Wilson for finding time to read and comment on the manuscript, in whole or in part, and so often saving me from myself. (Special thanks to the profs from El Cerrito for their unstinting support!) As ever I remain in debt to my fellow writers, friends and family, who are too many to name, for encouragement, practical help (especially via comments on the original cover art), and good counsel. Giving big ups as ever to Rethabile Masilo and Geoffrey Philp, for providing Internet spaces that celebrate poetry and featured poems from *de book of Mary*. Finally, I must thank Nurjehan Aziz and M. G. Vasanji for taking on board at Mawenzi House this radical retelling of an ancient story.

Some of the poems from this book previously appeared in the following places:

"Mary Telling Joseph that She Pregnant" in *ArtsEtc Barbados Special Issue*, May 2015 Kamau 85 http://www.artsetcbarbados.com/poetry/mary-telling-joseph-she-pregnant

"Mary, at Home, Thinking Further on Things" appeared in *Prism International* 53.2 Winter 2015. Print.

"Archangel Gabriel," "Mary, Confused," "Archangel Explains" and "Mary, Still Confused" appeared in *The Humber Literary Review* October 2015. Print.

"Miss Ann's Reaction When Mary Confesses" appeared on Rethabile Masilo's blogspot, Poéfrika http://poefrika.blogspot.ca/2015/01/miss-annes-reaction-when-mary-confesses.html

"Jesus Takes Leave of Mary and Goes into the Desert" appeared on Geoff Philp's blogspot http://geoffreyphilp.blogspot.ca/2015/08/excerpt-from-de-book-of-mary-by-pamela.html

"Mary pleads with Jah-Jah for guidance," "Advised by an angel, Joseph takes Mary as his wife," "Anna's prophecy," and "Jesus gives John to Mary as a son" appeared in *Canopic Jar: An Arts Journal* online at canopicjar.com/featured-voices/pam-mordecai/

Space does not permit me to enumerate all the websites on which I found material and all the books I consulted in writing *de book of Mary*. However, I must mention two books in particular. Stephanie Nolen's *28: Stories of Aids in Africa* (Toronto: Vintage Canada, 2008) gave me a vivid, moving introduction to persons living with AIDS in Africa. I especially thank Martin for finding *The Lost Books of the Bible*, compiled by William Hone (Konecky and Konecky, 2010; originally published NY: Alpha House, 1926). Out of these lost books came much that enriched my envisioning of Mary's story. One website also deserves particular mention, biblehub.com. The 22 versions of the Gospels (especially the Gospel of Matthew) that it affords were invaluable.

Pamela Mordecai writes poetry, fiction, and drama. Her previous collections of poetry are *Subversive Sonnets*, *The True Blue of Islands*, *Certifiable*, *de man: a performance poem*, and *Journey Poem*. Her first collection of short fiction, *Pink Icing and Other Stories*, appeared in 2006, and her first novel, *Red Jacket*, was published in February 2015 and shortlisted for the Rogers Writers' Trust Fiction Prize. Her writing for children is widely collected and well known internationally. *El Numero Uno*, a play for young people, had its world premiere at the Lorraine Kimsa Theatre for Young People in Toronto in 2010. She lives in Kitchener, Ontario.